Your Story Matters

Finding Purpose in God's Story

Steve and Marjie Schaefer

ISBN: 978-1-7328977-9-3

Cover Design: Lisa McKenney
Interior Layout and Design: Kristi Knowles

© 2024 by Steve and Marjie Schaefer. All rights reserved. No part of this document may be reproduced or transmitted in any form by any means, electronic, mechanical, photocopying, recording, or otherwise, without prior written permission of Steve and Marjie Schaefer.

"Blessed be the God and Father of our Lord Jesus Christ, who according to His abundant mercy has begotten us again to a living hope through the resurrection of Jesus Christ from the dead, to an inheritance incorruptible and undefiled and that does not fade away, reserved in heaven for you, who are kept by the power of God through faith for salvation ready to be revealed in the last time."

1 Peter 1:3-5

Contents

Beginning. 11

    Christ in the New 23

Middle 65

    Christ in the Old 75

End 119

Bible Study Resources for Women. 132

Preface

For the past fifteen years, my wife Marjie has written and taught many Bible studies as part of her leading the *Flourish Through the Word* women's ministry (see the back for more information regarding her Bible study resources).

One such teaching was on the book of Habakkuk, which she entitled *Your Story Matters*. Habakkuk's relevant story for today forms the framework for the following collection of devotionals: Our beginning, middle, and end.

Where I've pulled from Marjie's past teachings, I've prefaced each with the title she used for that particular Bible study.

Fortunately, Marjie's approach is to write out her lessons, so I'm grateful her teachings have been preserved. While always wanting to maintain the integrity of her lessons, I have, at times, taken some literary license when converting her lessons into brief devotionals. I have her permission for this, contingent upon purchasing a bouquet of peonies.

Given our emphasis on the Old Testament book of Habakkuk, we thought we'd flip things around and start with the New Testament devotionals first, concluding with the Old before we end.

Whether Old or New, all Scripture points to the person of Jesus Christ, so our intention is you'll see Him from Genesis to Revelation, for Christ is the scarlet thread of redemption woven throughout.

To that end, may you be drawn closer to the person of Jesus through these writings, for in Him *Your Story Matters*.

Steve
July 2024

Introduction

In full transparency, I confess to skimming over the bulk of names whenever I encounter a genealogy in the Bible. There, I've said it. Now, I have nothing against the folks who found their way onto the pages of Scripture, but most I can't pronounce, and even more I've never heard of. And with no ill will against Hodiah's wife or the sons of Shimon and Ishi, 2 Chronicles 4:19-20 is a simple example of my perpetual genealogical struggle:

> *"The sons of Hodiah's wife, the sister of Naham, were the fathers of Keilah the Garmite and of Eshtemoa the Maachathite. And the sons of Shimon were Amnon, Rinnah, Ben-Hanan, and Tilon. And the sons of Ishi were Zoheth and Ben-Zoheth."*

To me, they are just unrecognizable names on a very long list of unrecognizable names. Irrelevant for the lot of us, I suppose. Yet, upon reflection, I realize all these names were real people with actual lives. Each life like our own, experiencing birthdays, friendships, laughter, disappointment, interests, concerns, fear, grief, pain, joy, love, suffering, births, weddings, and death. Each one having a story. And like every story, each one having a beginning, middle, and end.

What gives a life story purpose? For the believer who confesses Jesus Christ as their Savior and Lord, ultimate purpose is intertwined with their communion and connection to Him.

While our lives will never appear in the Bible, and the bulk of us will soon be forgotten as the years pass by, the amazing truth is that God cares about each of us. Known or unknown. Visible in the public eye or hidden in anonymity. For every child is a chosen thread intertwined into the tapestry of His family, resulting in every son and daughter vital in God's master plan and design for His glory (Ephesians 2:1-10).

Paul framed this truth in terms of a body and its members (1 Corinthians 12). Each member necessary and united to the whole, and each member organically connected to their Head, Jesus Christ. So, given this reality, in the words of the title to Francis Schaeffer's book, *How Should We Then Live?*

The answer is found in a relatively obscure book of the Old Testament, a prophet by the name of Habakkuk. Eight little words from God found nestled in the second chapter: *"But the just shall live by his faith"* (Habakkuk 2:4). By faith. From beginning to end. It's the gift given to us by God when He resurrected us from the dead,

> *"And you He made alive, who were dead in trespasses and sins... For by grace you have been saved through faith, and that not of yourselves; it is the gift of God"* (Ephesians 2:1, 8).

And it's how we live out the remainder of our days here on earth,

> *"I have been crucified with Christ; it is no longer I who live, but Christ lives in me; and the life which I now live in the flesh I live by faith in the Son of God, who loved me and gave Himself for me"* (Galatians 2:20).

Whether you have faith the size of a tiny mustard seed (Matthew 17:20), or great centurion-like faith (Matthew 8:8-13), faith is the defining factor that sets you apart and makes your story one that truly matters.

Nowhere in the Bible is this more clearly articulated than in Hebrews chapter eleven. Nicknamed the great "Hall of Faith" chapter, here we read one faith story after another. Why concentrate and emphasize so many stories about faith? The sixth verse in this chapter tells us plainly,

> *"But without faith it is impossible to please Him, for he who comes to God must believe that He is, and that He is a rewarder of those who diligently seek Him."*

Simply put, faith pleases God. Trusting Him pleases Him. This is why Paul would instruct, *"For we walk by faith, not by sight"* (2 Corinthians 5:7), and would quickly add, *"Therefore we make it our aim, whether present or absent, to be well pleasing to Him"* (2 Corinthians 5:9). Faith and God's pleasure go hand-in-hand.

While you're not included in the stories of Hebrews chapter eleven, your story of faith matters—a story of faith only He can write. So until your story comes to its end, remain *"looking unto Jesus, the author and finisher of our faith"* (Hebrews 12:2).

Beginning

"I felt that I had been born anew and that the gates of heaven had been opened. The whole of Scripture gained a new meaning. And from that point on the phrase, 'the justice of God' no longer filled me with hatred, but rather became unspeakable sweet by virtue of a great love."

Martin Luther

Your Story Matters: Habakkuk

"O Lord, how long shall I cry and You will not hear? Even cry out to You, 'Violence!' and You will not save. Why do You cause me to see trouble?" (Habakkuk 1:2-3).

If ever there was a book in the Bible applicable for today, it's Habakkuk. Burrowed obscurely within the Old Testament's minor prophets, this little three-chapter book written more than 2,500 years ago deals with surprisingly modern problems: social unrest, political dysfunction, rampant evil, wars, and rumors of wars. Sound familiar? And terms that resonant with our lives today: *"The law is powerless... justice never goes forth... iniquity... violence... the wicked surround the righteous... perverse judgment proceeds."* Truly, there is nothing new under the sun.

Throughout this devotional, we will study this book as we examine its relevance to our perilous times. I encourage you to read all three chapters now as we begin. As we eavesdrop on this ancient story, this journey will reveal rich treasure and much for us to glean. And, while this study of God's Word could have been entitled "Trusting God in Troubled Times" or "Perplexities of a Puzzled Prophet," in the end, we've chosen "Your Story Matters" because your story is intertwined and connected to His story—the story of Jesus. How you and I respond to all that is happening in our world today will impact others for the sake of the Gospel and His Kingdom: God's advancing purposes on earth.

Why is that? Because despite the tumult, chaos, and evil of our world, you have Jesus. Jesus Christ is your life; all authority in heaven and earth has been given to Him, and now you have access to peace that surpasses all understanding. Christ in you, the hope of glory. And His Word tells you each day you go from strength to strength and glory to glory. This is the message you can impart to those the Lord puts in your path. Sharing the love of Christ with the next person God brings into your arena of influence. For your story matters.

Your Story Matters: God is in Control

"Look among the nations and watch – be utterly astounded! For I will work in your days which you would not believe, though it were told you. For indeed I am raising up the Chaldeans" (Habakkuk 1:5-6).

In this back-and-forth conversation between Habakkuk and God, we see the prophet's lament and God's response right at the start. Paraphrased, it goes something like this: "Lord, it's bad here in Judah. Do something!" "Ok, I'll do something. I'm going to send the Chaldeans to wipe out your nation." I think in today's vernacular, that would be called a giant curveball for Habakkuk. Not the answer he was expecting or hoping for.

The Chaldeans were a semi-nomadic tribe living in what is now Iraq. They were intelligent, aggressive, and warlike. In 626 B.C., Nabopolassar began an extended period where a Chaldean king ruled Babylon. During this time, the word "Chaldean" became synonymous with Babylon. The struggle between Judah and Babylon started in 605 B.C. when King Nebuchadnezzar forced Judah and King Jehoiakim to be his servants. Several puppet kings and rebellions later, the Babylonians had had enough, destroying Judah in 586 B.C. It was during this period leading up to the fall of Judah when Habakkuk was written.

The macro and the micro: God raising up and tearing down nations, while also having an intimate and personal dialogue with Habakkuk. Here's what Martyn Lloyd-Jones had to say about the former:

> "Every nation on earth is under the Hand of God, for there is no power in this world that is not ultimately controlled by Him. Things are not what they appear to be. It seemed that it was the military prowess of the Chaldeans that brought them up…. but it was not so at all, for God had raised them up. God is the Lord of history. He is seated in the heavens, and the nations to Him are as 'grasshoppers,' as a drop in the bucket, or as small dust of the balance. He started the historical process, and He is controlling it, and He is going to end it. We must never lose sight of this crucial fact."

Your Story Matters: A Part of His Story

"Are You not from everlasting, O Lord my God, my Holy One?"
(Habakkuk 1:12).

God has an ongoing conversation with His beloved Habakkuk. The prophet, in response, addresses Him as *"my God, my Holy One."* So very intimate and personal. God at the micro level with His chosen ones. Here is Habakkuk, whose very name means "embrace," embraced by God and embracing, as we will see in chapter three, the challenging future ahead. May we, too, embrace all that God has for us in His Word, embracing those around us, taking on the mantle of an encourager as we walk out our faith in the days that lie ahead.

So, does your story matter? You bet it does! God uses your personal story and sovereignly weaves it into His larger story of the Kingdom. At the end of the day, it's all about Him, it's all about trust, and it's all about worship – regardless of what you may think or feel. God is in control, and He will make a way when there seems to be no way. Can you embrace the things in your life that God is, or is not, currently doing or is allowing to happen? Can you say with Habakkuk by faith, *"… yet I will rejoice in the Lord. I will joy in the God of my salvation."* As Henri Nouwen writes about the micro:

> "The great spiritual battle begins – and never ends – with the reclaiming of our chosenness. Long before any human being saw us, we are seen by God's loving eyes. Long before anyone heard us cry or laugh, we are heard by our God who is all ears for us. Long before any person spoke to us in this world, we are spoken to by the voice of eternal love. Our preciousness, uniqueness, and individuality are not given to us by those who meet us in clock-time – our brief chronological existence – but by the One who has chosen us with an everlasting love, a love that existed from all eternity and will last through all eternity."

Your Story Matters: Habakkuk 1

"The burden which the prophet Habakkuk saw" (Habakkuk 1:1).

How often do we *see* burdens? We often feel burdens, but here we read that the prophet is actually seeing the burden. Like Habakkuk, we need spiritual eyes to respond and not react to the burdens and difficulties around us. Reacting involves getting anxious, angry, worked up, flustered, or fearful about the things we see, whereas responding is a more thoughtful and prayerful approach to the burdens, troubles, and situations that arise around us. 1 Thessalonians 5:23 is a beautiful verse to help us in processing such turbulence in our lives:

> *"And may the God of peace Himself sanctify you through and through (separate you from profane things, make you pure and wholly consecrated to God); and may your spirit and soul and body be preserved sound and complete and found blameless at the coming of our Lord Jesus Christ."*

This verse reveals a divine order in our lives: spirit, soul, and body. Our spirit is meant to dominate our soul, which is meant to dominate our body. Only God's Holy Spirit, taking up residence in our spirit, can return our souls to a modicum of wholeness and health God intended prior to sin entering the world. Apart from His presence in our spirit, our soul – made up of our mind, will, and emotions – will dominate, and our emotions will often cause us to react to life rather than respond in a Spirit-dominated way.

Even King David had to tell his soul to behave when he said, *"Bless the Lord, O my soul!"* (Psalm 103:2). Our souls don't always respond how we would like them to – so sometimes we have to tell them! The Lord desires that we be led by His Holy Spirit (Galatians 5:16-18), living out our lives in His divine order so that our spirit, soul, and body would *be preserved sound and complete and found blameless* when our faith turns to sight, and we see Jesus.

Your Story Matters: Bad Moon Rising

"For indeed I am raising up the Chaldeans" (Habakkuk 1:6).

"O Lord, how long shall I cry and You will not hear? Even cry out to You, 'Violence!' and You will not save" (v. 2). How long do you think it was? Months? Years? And nothing. Evil just kept going on and on and on. Iniquity, trouble, violence, strife, contention, injustice, perverse judgment, and wickedness flourishing, and God apparently doing nothing about it. Why won't God do something?!? But at last, Habakkuk gets his long-awaited (but unexpected) answer to prayer. The answer is the Chaldeans.

"A bitter and hasty nation…..they are terrible and dreadful" (v. 6-7). With horses *"swifter than leopards, and more fierce than evening wolves"* (v. 8), conquering nations left and right, this extreme and powerful realm will now have their sights set on Judah. There you have it……God finally answered the prophet's prayer. The bad guys are coming, and God tells Habakkuk He is the One who is responsible and that *He* will do it. On purpose. By design.

Unanswered prayer. Answers we didn't ask for or want. In this case, a more wicked nation raised up to defeat one relatively less. How do we comport our understanding of a good and loving God with His answer to Habakkuk? And a little closer to home, what about the person constantly working against you and mispresenting something you've done or said? Why does God allow this person to succeed? Or suppose you experience some great disappointment – the death of a child or spouse, the breakup of a marriage or engagement, failure to get the job or into the program you want. Doesn't God care? Of course you're not perfect, but why should someone who doesn't love Jesus have things go so well for them when you've been left to struggle with your disappointment and grief?

These quandaries of the soul are at the very heart of Habakkuk. From *Disappointment with God* by Philip Yancy:

> "Why the delay? Why does God let evil and pain so flagrantly exist, even thrive, on this planet? He holds back for our sakes. Re-creation involves us; we are, in fact, at the center of his plan... the motive behind all human history, is to develop us, not God. Our very existence announces to the powers in the universe that restoration is underway. Every act of faith by every one of the people of God is like the tolling of a bell, and a faith like Job's reverberates throughout the universe."

Your Story Matters: Laboring for the Revelation

"I... do not cease to give thanks for you, making mention of you in my prayers: that the God of our Lord Jesus Christ, the Father of glory, may give you the spirit of wisdom and revelation in the knowledge of Him..."
(Ephesians 1:15-17).

So many times, when people face difficult things, as a coping mechanism they choose to withdraw from their Christian friends. They stop going to church, reading their Bibles, and potentially go as far as to think they were wrong about God, with many renouncing their belief in Him. We've all seen it happen and maybe felt it ourselves. So what can we do – in advance – to help resist this human tendency? For if we're to build a house on the rock, we need to do so *before* the rain, floods, and winds of life come against us.

We'd like to offer several practical applications to help build a framework for responding (vs. reacting) to disturbing or unsettling events that transpire in our lives. The first is *Stop and Think*. When difficult things happen, we tend to talk first and think later. The book of James tells us, *"Everyone should be quick to listen, slow to speak"* (James 1:19). When we allow our mouths to run away with our brains, we can fan the flames of our own unbelief, muddling our thinking. When we stop to think first, we begin to sort things out and allow the light of God to shine on our situation. What do we know to be true about God, His Word, and His care of His people? God is always good, and we are always loved!

Second, we need to *Restate Basic Truth*. When we stop and think, don't begin with the immediate problem. Be a good historian and start further back, getting the entire context of a loving God who deals with us righteously. *"I will remember the works of the Lord; surely I will remember Your wonders of old"* (Psalm 77:11). This is called finding sound footing. Here's a word picture to illustrate: Have you ever walked on a sidewalk in the winter when the snow was cleared off, but it was still treacherous due to icy spots? What did you do? Most likely, you kept your eyes down and placed your feet carefully on the safe ground that was clear of ice. In the same way, Habakkuk finds himself in a spiritual "slippery spot" – but surely his entire experience with God is not like what he is currently hearing. We'll see how Habakkuk soon gets onto the firm parts. He will begin to remind himself of things he knows to be true. As he does, the dilemma starts to fall into proper perspective. For God is always good, and we are always loved!

Your Story Matters: Laboring for the Revelation (continued)

"But the just shall live by his faith" (Habakkuk 2:4).

Finally, *Commit the Problem to God in Faith* and leave it in His hands. Suppose you have stopped to think, you've restated basic truths and applied them to the problem, but you still find the difficulty confronting you. In Habakkuk's case, the wicked Chaldeans are still coming, and God Himself is raising them up to judge the nation of Judah. What do you do? Do you give up? Do you withdraw and hide in a closet? Do you renounce your belief and faith in a loving God? Or do you leave the matter with God and simply trust Him because He's trustworthy?

While simple never implies easy, faith says, "Lord, I've done everything I know to do with this problem or situation, and I still don't understand it even though I've faced it based on everything I know to be true in Your Word. So while I still don't understand, and while I still don't know what to do, my eyes are on You." This is belief, and this is trust. And this is precisely what God wants us to do, for Peter says we are to be *"casting all your care upon Him, for He cares for you"* (1 Peter 5:7).

Speaking of Peter, there was a time when Jesus had been preaching, and His followers were increasing. But then he started preaching some very hard things (John 6). To the point where *"... many of His disciples went back and walked with Him no more"* (John 6:66). Turning to the twelve, Jesus asked them, *"Do you also want to go away?"* (John 6:67). Peter answered, *"Lord, to whom shall we go? You have the words of eternal life"* (John 6:68). We've all probably been there in our lives. Maybe you're there right now. Confused and perplexed by the hard things God has allowed, wondering if the trial will end. But press into Jesus, labor for the revelation, reflect on what you know is true from His Word, and you will realize there is no one else but Him – He is the Truth of your situation, and He has the words of eternal life. For there is no life apart from Jesus.

As Philip Yancy wrote in *Disappointment with God*: "Faith means believing in advance what will only make sense in reverse."

Your Story Matters: He Gave Us Jesus

"He who did not spare His own Son, but delivered Him up for us all, how shall He not with Him also freely give us all things?" (Romans 8:32).

We don't know why anyone dies tragically or suddenly—especially those in the prime of youth or those doing amazing things for God and His Kingdom. And we don't know all the reasons why God allows evil and suffering in our world to continue or why it's sometimes so apparently random in society, but at least we know what the reason is *not* – what it can't be. It can't be that He doesn't love us. It can't be that He doesn't care.

Identifying as a Christian and believing in Jesus means we know God came to earth in the form of a man and became subject to suffering and death Himself, dying on the cross to take the punishment our sins deserved. He is so committed to us that He was willing to plunge into the greatest depths of grief and pain Himself. Suffering so He might be sympathetic (Hebrews 4:15), dying so we might have life abundantly (John 10:10). Jesus truly understands our earthly plight and assures us He has a plan to eventually wipe away every tear from our eyes, making everything sad become untrue.

Yes, one day, He will return and will end all suffering. Without ending us. But for now, like a 3-year-old who cannot understand most of what their parents allow and don't allow for them, that same child can understand their parents' love, trust them, and live securely. In the same way, as we filter all of life through the cross and the gospel of Jesus Christ, we too can be assured and reassured of our Father's unchanging love for us. As Anne Voskamp wrote in *One Thousand Gifts*:

> "God gave us Jesus… if God didn't withhold from us His very own Son, will God withhold anything we need? If trust must be earned, hasn't God unequivocally earned our trust with the bark on the raw wounds, the thorns pressed into the brow, your name on the cracked lips? How will He not also graciously give us all things He deems best and right? He's already given the incomprehensible."

Your Story Matters: Habakkuk's Response

"Are You not from everlasting, O Lord my God, my Holy One? We shall not die. O Lord, You have appointed them for judgment; O Rock, you have marked them for correction" (Habakkuk 1:12).

Rather than reacting, Habakkuk found solid footing by reminding himself of the most basic and fundamental truths—namely, the attributes of God. Long before anything came into existence, and long after the Chaldeans would cease to exist, He would be. Even if Habakkuk could not understand all God was doing during his lifetime, he would find profound comfort in knowing he served the *everlasting* God.

And then Habakkuk speaks to the most overarching characteristic of God – His *holiness*. In the Bible, it is an attribute stressed more than any other. Again and again, God reminds us of His holy name. It is the only attribute repeated three times on several occasions – *"Holy, Holy, Holy is the Lord God Almighty"* (Isaiah 6:3; Revelation 4:8). The absolute purity of God, and the absolute distance between God and sinful humanity. Next, Habakkuk acknowledges God's *sovereignty*. He alone rules over His creation. He alone appoints those destined for judgment, and He alone marks the Chaldeans for correction. Finally, the prophet declares God's faithfulness by calling Him a *Rock*. God, the Rock, is a place of security for His people. He is a foundation on which we can build a secure dwelling, and He is a fortress a soldier can run into and find safety.

So Habakkuk stopped and thought; he restated the truth, and now he applied it to his current predicament. He must have thought, "If God is the everlasting God – if He was here before anything we know came into existence and will be here after all our problems and enemies have faded away – then the Chaldean invasion will not be His last word – however daunting and final that invasion may be for me. If God is holy and sovereign, then the outcome of this invasion will not be evil but will ultimately achieve some good purpose. And if God is faithful, then a Chaldean victory must be for the ultimate good of His people, for He will not abandon us. We will always be His people."

As believers possessing *"the mind of Christ"* (1 Corinthians 2:16) and filled with His Spirit, we have been enabled to think God's thoughts after Him. Like Habakkuk, we too have all we need to respond.

Your Story Matters: Worship in the Face of Calamity

"Are You not from everlasting, O Lord my God, my Holy One? We shall not die. O Lord, You have appointed them for judgment; O Rock, you have marked them for correction" (Habakkuk 1:12).

As Habakkuk processes this startling news from God, he moves toward the one thing that will give him a solid footing in the complex, confusing, and scary days that lie ahead: The worship of the Living God. True worship is unconditional; it's not an attempt to manipulate God but rather changes and shapes *us*, positioning us for all God is doing in His story and in ours. Psalm 22:3 says, *"But You are holy, enthroned in the praises of Israel."* In other words, God lives in our very praises. When we praise, we enthrone God over our lives and circumstances. Psalm 50:23 says,

"He who sacrifices thank offerings honors Me, and he prepares the way so that I may show him the salvation of God."

The idea of sacrificing thank offerings includes thanking and praising Him when you've received bad news or feel trapped in difficult circumstances. Yes, even when you don't feel like it.

Through worship, we focus on God Himself. Not the problem. We see Habakkuk arriving at this exact spot in chapter one. We see him starting to focus on God rather than the impending invasion. When we fix our eyes on Him, our praise begins to spring from a simple response of faith—the choice to believe God. Even in troubled circumstances, or when God doesn't choose to work in a spectacular way (as we define *spectacular*), worship gives us a different lens to view our circumstances. This is part of responding vs. reacting. This is allowing our spirits to dominate our souls.

Worship and praise tune out the conflicting voices attempting to shatter our faith and block His love. They also tune us into God's guidance so we can discern His voice and any action He would have us take. God's plan for us all is not that we live lives of struggle and defeat but rather victory. To thrive and not just survive. Within the trial. Prior to deliverance. Isaiah 64:5 says, *"You meet him who rejoices."* Don't you want Him to meet with you? For when He does, you too will be able to face your own Chaldeans.

Christ in the New

"You search the Scriptures, for in them you think you have eternal life; and these are they which testify of Me. But you are not willing to come to Me that you may have life"
(John 5:39-40).

The Great Exchange

"Christ has redeemed us from the curse of the law, having become a curse for us...., that the blessing of Abraham might come upon the Gentiles in Christ Jesus, that we might receive the promise of the Spirit through faith" (Galatians 3:13-14).

The word *redeemed* means "to gain possession of something or someone, in exchange for payment." What a beautiful description of the finished work of Christ and of the sons and daughters who His blood has purchased. As John the Baptist declared at Christ's baptism, *"Behold! The Lamb of God who takes away the sin of the world!"* (John 1:29). Becoming our spotless Passover Lamb, the Father's firstborn Son was without blemish or defect. Not only did Christ fulfill all the righteous requirements of the law and liberate us from the curse of it, He also once and for all put an end to the sacrificial system by being God's perfect substitutionary offering.

But the substitution didn't end there. Jesus Christ is alive today to be your substitution. The great exchange is still taking place! His confidence for your apprehension. His strength for your weakness. His wisdom for your confusion. His comfort for your grief. His peace for your anxiety. His provision for your lack. His companionship for your loneliness. His ability for your inability. His presence for your fear. His freedom for your bondage. His grace for your guilt. His _____ for your _____. You fill in the blank. What do you need today? He is the One who meets you right where you are and gives you what you need to get through the day, the stress, the difficulty, the hard season, the divorce, the wayward child, the unemployment, the semester, the surgery, and even the diagnosis.

Jesus will always be your great strength in all your many weaknesses, for He lives to be your daily substitution.

Received Not Achieved

"As you therefore have received Christ Jesus the Lord, so walk in Him, rooted and built up in Him and established in the faith, as you have been taught, abounding in it with thanksgiving" (Colossians 2:6-7).

In John chapter 8, we are told the story of the woman caught in the very act of adultery. What a perfect picture of who we were and what we brought to the table when Christ appeared in our lives. Like us, the woman didn't do anything to get right with God. Please note the woman had not even repented! She is just standing there in her guilt – she was caught in the act. She didn't clean up her life first, she didn't go on a short-term mission trip, she didn't get her purse to pay her tithes and offerings, and she most definitely was not the perfect spouse. She just vulnerably stood before Jesus and anticipated He too would condemn and accuse her like all the other religious people she was surrounded by. But instead, Jesus asks her, *"Where are those accusers of yours? Has no one condemned you?"* (John 8:10). That's what the law does. It accuses and condemns, revealing our guilt before a Holy God and producing shame in us. The same shame that drove Adam and Eve to foolishly hide from God in the garden. And we've been foolishly hiding in our shame ever since.

But in Christ, there is no condemnation, *"neither do I condemn you......"* while adding, *"......go and sin no more"* (John 8:11). While Jesus does not accuse or condemn, He does not excuse or condone sin either. His will is for us to know and experience the life He has for us – the abundant life – the life of faith, fullness, freedom, joy, and peace. Jesus knows continuing in sin will rob us of the very life he died to give us. This is why Jesus immediately provided the woman with a resource to help her: Himself. *"I am the light of the world. He who follows Me shall not walk in darkness, but have the light of life"* (John 8:12).

Already Complete

"For in Him dwells all the fullness of the Godhead bodily; and you are complete in Him, who is the head of all principality and power" (Colossians 2:9-10).

At the end of the hit 1996 movie *Jerry Maguire*, Tom Cruise (Jerry) declared his love to Renee Zellweger (Dorothy) with the immortalized words, *"You complete me."* While the romantic within us may swoon at the apparent passionate bliss shared between Jerry and Dorothy, upon deeper reflection, is that what *true love* really is? I'd say an emphatic no. In fact, what the sentiment conveys is, unfortunately, quite the opposite of love: With needy eyes, Jerry, in essence, says, "You *complete me because I need to be completed; I'm incomplete without you. Therefore, I choose to be with you because being with you is about me and my needs. My wants. My feelings. My inadequacies. And that is why I value you."*

In contrast to Hollywood, the Bible says in Jesus you have everything you need to get through this day, this week, this year, and this season of life. You are already complete in Him. The enemy of your soul desperately does not want you to believe this. He will repeatedly lie, whispering you are incomplete and doomed to a life of struggle unless you have this, that, or the other thing. You need a spouse to be complete. You need to own a home, have children, attain a specific title at work or in the church, make a certain amount of money, or have friends to become complete.

But the word of God says differently. It says if you are in Christ, then you are already complete. Christ is sufficient. He alone is enough. Christ in you, the hope of glory, is what completes, empowers, transforms, and enables you. As Asaph understood when penning Psalm 73:25, *"Whom have I in heaven but You? And there is none upon earth that I desire besides You."* Like him, we too can now declare, *"Jesus, You alone complete me."*

O the Deep, Deep Love of Jesus

"Having loved His own who were in the world, He loved them to the end"
(John 13:1).

    The love of Jesus is not a flash in the pan. It does not begin with a bang and then slowly recede over the course of time should His sons and daughters drift, compromise, and sin. On the other hand, human love has its limitations, such as retracting when betrayed. Growing cold when abandoned. Embittered when forsaken. Whereas our love has a constriction point, the love of Jesus loves to the end. Not only is He the author of your faith, but He's the finisher also. So, what does loving to the end look like?

    John 13:1 begins the final week of life on earth for Jesus. Up until that point, His three-year earthly ministry had been no cakewalk. He was misunderstood, mistreated, tired, hungry, cornered, and accused. However, what lay behind was nothing compared to what lay ahead. He was about to be betrayed by a close friend. Abandoned by all the disciples. Tortured by His accusers. And yet, even these would all pale compared to His impending death. For if He was sweating blood at the *thought* of God's abandonment and judgment (Luke 22:44), what would it be like to go through with it? Forsaken by His Father on the cross, the cumulative absorption of God's focused wrath for every sin committed over the many centuries by all His people would soon be directed at Him. This is what it means to love to the end.

    From the hymn *O The Deep, Deep Love of Jesus:*

O the deep, deep love of Jesus, vast unmeasured, boundless free
Rolling as a mighty ocean in its fullness over me.
Underneath me, all around me, is the current of His love
Leading onward, leading homeward, to my glorious rest above.

There is a Fountain

"Indeed, under the law almost everything is purified with blood, and without the shedding of blood there is no forgiveness of sin" (Hebrews 9:22).

Many years ago, Marjie took a relative of ours to Bible Study Fellowship to hear the message. The study that day was on the crucifixion of Jesus Christ and what it was like to die on a Roman cross from a medical perspective. After returning to the car, this relative was extremely upset, yelling at Marjie for having brought her to such a horrific message. She found it extremely upsetting for the teacher to have gone into such excruciating detail about the pain and suffering of Christ during His execution. She told Marjie never to ask her again to go, a request Marjie would honor. *"For the message of the cross is foolishness to those who are perishing, but to us who are being saved it is the power of God"* (1 Corinthians 1:18).

In the spirit of complete transparency, I am not filled with eager anticipation when I see the book of Leviticus approaching in my Bible reading plan. And yet, in this book, we see our need for the shedding of blood ever so clearly. A Holy God and sinful people. Eighty-seven times in this book, the word "holiness" appears, while "blood" is mentioned 82 times, the word "sacrifice" 50, and "offering" over 300 times. The death and crucifixion of Jesus Christ was not just any execution. Christ's death was the perfect sacrifice, fulfilling the myriads of precise specifications detailed in the book of Leviticus, bridging sinful man to a Holy God. *"For by one offering He has perfected forever those who are being sanctified"* (Hebrews 10:14). The cross was not a horrific tragedy of death, but a glorious triumph bringing life to those who see their need for the shedding of blood.

From the hymn *There is a Fountain:*

> *There is a fountain filled with blood drawn from Immanuel's veins*
> *And sinners plunged beneath that flood lose all their guilty stains*
> *Dear dying Lamb thy precious blood shall never lose its power*
> *Till all the ransomed Church of God be saved to sin no more*

The Lost Art of Curiosity

"Let each of you look out not only for his own interests, but also for the interests of others. Let this mind be in you which was also in Christ Jesus…"
(Philippians 2:4,5).

In this ever-increasing online, polarized, and lonely world in which we live, it seems dialogue and healthy conversations have gone the way of the dinosaurs. Living at a time when things seem to be spiraling out of control, now more than ever, we need to pour Jesus out into a hurting world. One very practical way we can love our neighbor and pour out Jesus is by showing a genuine interest in others. Here are some simple (but not easy!) steps you can take to become a better conversationalist:

- **Have a one-conversation rule.** Put all your devices away and focus on the one strand of conversation.
- **Listen with your heart.** There is a big difference between letting the other person talk so you can reload versus listening to truly learn about and understand the other person.
- **Be aware of how much you are talking.** Less is more. Studies have shown that, on average, we have 3.6 blind spots, so ask the Holy Spirit to help you become more alert to this.
- **Hit the ball back over the net.** If someone asks you a question (How was your summer?), respond, and then ask them the same question.
- **Ask follow-up questions.** Be curious, and then follow your curiosity. Follow-up questions reveal so much more of a person's story and show a genuine interest in them and their interests.
- **Provide positive feedback through your body language and tone when conversing.** Research by Albert Mehrabian found that communication is 55% nonverbal, 38% tonal, and only 7% words. One time, the pastor who met me kept looking over my shoulder in hopes there was someone —anyone—other than me he could talk to. In addition to eye contact, another practice is *heart-to-heart,* turning your physical heart towards the heart of the one you are conversing with. This conveys value and is a much different message than having your heart turned toward your computer, phone, or TV when someone is speaking to you.

A good rule of thumb for love: The most important person in the world is the person right in front of you.

This Little Light of Mine

"You are all children of the light...put on faith and love as a breastplate and the hope of salvation as a helmet" (1 Thessalonians 5:5,8).

The moon generates no light of its own but merely reflects the light of the sun. This is most evident during a total lunar eclipse, when the Moon moves into the Earth's shadow, blocking the sun's light. No sun……no moonlight. In the same way, you too are a reflector of the Son. Having no light of your own, the light you mirror is the light of Jesus, who is the Light of the World.

In the verse above, the fact you are *"children of the light"* is what is called an indicative statement. Meaning, it is a statement of fact. It *indicates* something. There is nothing for you to do but believe. If I say, "The car is in the garage," you either believe it……or you don't. So, do you believe you are a carrier of Light? On the other hand, *"put on faith and love as a breastplate and the hope of salvation as a helmet"* is an imperative statement. There is an action to be performed: *"put on……"* Christ in you has made you a light-giver, so how can you now prevent and ward off a total eclipse?

The imperative statement tells us how: faith, love, and hope. Faith and love make up our breastplate. When was the last time you wore a breastplate? Probably never, but it's akin to a Kevlar vest in our day and age. A breastplate protects your vital organs, primarily your heart. Faith (taking God at His Word) and love (serving others with care and compassion) act as a supernatural shield for your heart. And *"the hope of salvation"* is your helmet, becoming another supernatural guardian protecting your thought life. A spiritual covering for your mind. This *hope* is not only heaven but also a blueprint of the future God *"prepared beforehand"* (Ephesians 2:10) for you to walk in as an outcome of your salvation.

While the enemy of your soul cannot take away the light God has placed in you, he can – and will – attack your faith, love, and hope. So what are you to do? *"Watch, stand fast in the faith, be brave, be strong. Let all that you do be done with love"* (1 Corinthians 16:13-14).

Planted

"And let us consider one another in order to stir up love and good works, not forsaking the assembling of ourselves together, as is the manner of some, but exhorting one another; and so much more as you see the Day approaching" (Hebrews 10:24-25).

Remember the science project back in elementary school days where you would put a seed in some dirt, water it, and then leave it on a windowsill to grow? That first week, you would rush out every morning to see what new and miraculous events transpired while you slept, only to be gravely disappointed by the boring lack of activity. For the impatient among us, by day three or four, we were digging up the seed to see what might have gone wrong. Of course, now that we've matured and know the speed of photosynthesis, we can look back and enjoy a light-hearted chuckle at our more juvenile selves. And yet, have we changed, or have the opportunities for impatience and disappointment merely graduated to more adult-like activities?

Take, for instance, church attendance. How easy it is to "dig up the seed" before it has a chance to grow. While consumerism may be acceptable at the shopping mall or when ordering online, it is not who you are as a member of Christ's body. I've always believed that if good people come together to do good, bad things will invariably occur. That's just life. In families, at work, and in church. The sermons will go too long, the worship will be too loud, and there will be difficulties, misunderstandings, and offenses. But that's the point. God wants us in the mess to grow like Christ and learn what it truly means to love. And God practices what He preaches: Jesus came to our mess, walked among us, loved us, and remains with us through His Spirit.

And now, born anew, we are members of Christ's body, organically connected, one to the other. We are not marbles in a bag or books on a shelf, sharing close proximity but lacking connection. Instead, when a finger is cut and bleeding, the foot doesn't say, *"I'm out of here!"* It remains, for the human body is in it for the long haul…..together. In the same way, when you see a problem in the church, be the solution! In fact, seeing the gaps and problems is the very thing that qualifies you to *stay*, not leave. So allow your roots to go down deep, for *"Those who are planted in the house of the Lord shall flourish in the courts of our God"* (Psalm 92:13).

Never Give In

"Let us not grow weary or become discouraged in doing good, for at the proper time we will reap, if we do not give in" (Galatians 6:9).

On October 29th, 1941, Winston Churchill delivered an address to Harrow School. With the final phase of the German attack on Russia commencing earlier that same month, Churchill chose not to give his remarks on the BBC or to the House of Commons in Parliament, but to the students of his alma mater. In his message, Churchill exhorted the audience to:

"Never give in. Never give in. Never, never, never, never – in nothing, great or small, large or petty – never give in, except to convictions of honour and good sense. Never yield to force. Never yield to the apparently overwhelming might of the enemy."

To *give up* means to stop trying to do something. To *give in* means to stop trying to fight or resist an opposing force. At the height of Nazi domination and apparent overwhelming might, Churchill implored his people to *never yield*.

The same is true in spiritual warfare. While we tend to get the two mixed up, the Bible teaches us to flee youthful lusts and to fight the devil. So don't fight lust and run from the devil. Fight him! *"Stand against the wiles of the devil…. above all, taking up the shield of faith with which you will be able to quench all the fiery darts of the wicked one. And take….the sword of the Spirit, which is the word of God"* (Ephesians 6:11,16-17). Yes, we too are at war, but unlike WW II, ours is not against flesh and blood. And yet the admonition remains the same: Never give in.

When Logic Fails

"In a great trial of affliction, the abundance of their joy and their deep poverty abounded in the riches of their liberality" (2 Corinthians 8:2).

Data from the United States Census Bureau's 2023 American Community Survey shows Seattle ranked No. 1 among the nation's 50 most-populous cities for the percentage of those 25 and older with a college degree. Suffice it to say, the bulk of us living in this neck of the woods put a pretty high premium on our rational, scientific, and logical thought. And why this may serve us well in some capacities; in other ways, it may be our greatest weakness. Take giving and generosity, for example. Simple logic would tell us if I have earned, say, $100 and I have expenses totaling $100, I have a net amount left over of $0. When we take such logic into our relationship with God, read the above passage from 2 Corinthians, or read the account of the poor widow who gave all she had (Mark 12:41-44), it makes no sense to our rational mind. And yet this is the very juxtaposition laid out for us in Proverbs 3:5, *"Trust in the Lord with all of your heart, and lean not on your own understanding."* This is the tension. The contrast. The test. Which one will we choose?

If the poor widow had used her rationality when going to the treasury, she would have come to a much more logical conclusion than the one she did. She would have concluded God did not need her *"two small coins."* Besides, rationality would clearly say she required those two small coins to live on. Instead, it appears something else drove her. Like the Macedonian churches in 2 Corinthian 8 and 9, who in their poverty gave liberally, for they gave out of their love for God and their trust in Him. As Becky Tirabassi points out about the poor widow:

> "So much of the time we try to reason ourselves into obedience. But instead we should begin by reasoning from love. When obedience is based on love, it isn't a responsibility. It's a response. Jesus did not praise the poor widow for her clear logic about God's worthiness but for her deep love for God Himself."

Like the poor widow, from love, let's prioritize our trust in the Lord over our logic when it comes to money.

Pursuing the Intentional Life with Jesus

"And the things that you that you heard from me among many witnesses, commit these to faithful men who will be able to teach others also"
(2 Timothy 2:2).

    Here, Paul lays out for Timothy the pattern for spiritual parenting. While many may not have biological children, no matter where we are in our life's journey, there will always be someone younger who needs your wisdom, encouragement, input, and spiritual investment. The good news is this kind of encourager does not require a degree in counseling or seminary training; it merely requires a willingness to invest your life in serving Him and others. It requires living a deliberate life. And that begins with a pursuit of the intentional life with Jesus. Here are three specific ways we can pursue this life with Him:

1. **Make Jesus the Center of Your Life:** We often hear make Jesus number one, and while true, making Him the center of all that we are, say, and do is really the more accurate picture. Busyness plagues us all, so if we don't carve out a daily adequate pause and allow time spent with the Lord, we will miss the rhythm of life and may be set adrift without purpose and without Jesus at the center.
2. **Pray For and/or With Your 'Children' Every Day:** Whether you have physical or spiritual children, or both, one of the best ways we can pray for those we love is by praying God's Word for and over them. The longer I (Marjie) walk with Jesus, the more I realize how important prayer is because prayer is my conversation with Him – it's the vehicle for our relationship. With the Word of God as the centerpiece of my life with Jesus, as I pray it over others, I appeal to Him and His character to do what only He can do.
3. **Speak Words of Life and Gratitude:** *"Death and life are in the power of the tongue, and those who love it will eat its fruit"* (Proverbs 18:21). Life is hard enough as it is without the destructive force of our words tearing others down. Let's intentionally resolve like David to speak words of life, *"And my tongue shall speak of Your righteousness and of Your praise all the day long"* (Psalm 35:28).

    We are *all* in the generational relay race called life, and the baton we pass is the truth of God's Word, leading to faith in Jesus Christ.

Because of Envy

"But Pilate answered them, saying, 'Do you want me to release to you the King of the Jews?' For he knew that the chief priests had handed Him over because of envy" (Mark 15:9-10).

It seems the sin of envy doesn't quite hold the same weight or gravity it once did in our collective minds. In fact, brands such as Revlon, BMW, and Calvin Klein have widely used envy in their advertising campaigns. *"We're just trying to keep up with the Joneses,"* we might glibly say with a wry smirk. Defined as *a feeling of discontented or resentful longing aroused by someone else's possessions, qualities, or good fortune,* envy has become an approved societal norm for this materialistic age in which we live. And yet we see in Scripture, from a human perspective, this was the very sin that nailed Jesus to the cross.

The envious tipping point for these leaders to murder was twofold: the raising of Lazarus from the dead (John 11:28-44) and the triumphant entry of Christ into Jerusalem (John 12:12-15). The former was the last straw, *"Then, from that day on, they plotted to put Him to death"* (John 11:53), while the latter exposed their true envious wishes, *"Look, the world has gone after Him!"* (John 12:19). They wanted the whole world to go after them…. not Jesus! Try as they might to mask their true motivations; even the tyrant Pontius Pilate could see right through them.

Such is the nature of envy. While self-deluded justifications may abound in our minds and lips, envy is never hidden—from God or man. And though we may deminimize its grievous nature, God does not. He puts it alongside murder and sorcery in listing out the works of the flesh in Galatians 5:19-21. The antidote? Gratitude to God for the boundary lines He's drawn for us and others. Especially for others. Might this have been why Paul said he *"learned in whatever state I am, to be content"* (Philippians 4:11)? Contentment is learned, not birthed. So, let's learn and find great gratitude for our lot while rejoicing with those who have reason to rejoice. Even when they've received what we haven't. For envy is not a "respectable" sin to be trifled with.

Flourishing Friendships: Our Best Friend

"No longer do I call you servants.... I have called you friends" (John 15:15).

Bronnie Ware, in her book *The Top Five Regrets of the Dying*, noticed her patients in palliative care had a clarity of vision at the end of their lives. She asked them if they would do anything differently if they could go back. Frequently, many would say, *"I wish I had stayed in touch with my friends."* Bronnie explains:

> "Often, they would not truly realize the full benefits of old friends until their dying weeks, and it was not always possible to track them down. Many had become so caught up in their own lives that they let golden friendships slip by over the years. There were many deep regrets about not giving friendships the time and effort they deserved."

Unlike the patients above, we may not be in the final weeks of our lives. How wonderful it is that we are given the opportunity to restore what they could not. It's not too late. So where do we begin to rekindle a neglected friendship or one needing restoration? We start with the Friend who knows us better than anyone, better than we even know ourselves, and that Friend is Jesus.

Called a *"friend of sinners,"* Jesus is the One who lets us all the way in and loves us to the very end, always inviting us into His loving embrace extended to all who know Him. Drawing near to Him we discover the greatest power for becoming a better friend is being befriended by our best Friend. On the eve of His death, Jesus wanted His disciples – His friends – to know the cross was not only the greatest demonstration of love the world has ever seen, but also the greatest act of friendship, *"Greater love has no one than this, that someone lay down his life for His friends"* (John 15:13). As believers in Christ, we have been immersed into the Trinitarian community of love between the Father, Son, and Holy Spirit. To be a Christian is to know Jesus – and to be known by Him – as a dear friend.

From the hymn *What a Friend We Have in Jesus:*

> *What a Friend we have in Jesus, all our sins and griefs to bear.*
> *What a privilege to carry everything to God in prayer.*
> *O what peace we often forfeit, O what needless pain we bear,*
> *All because we do not carry everything to God in prayer.*

Flourishing Friendships: Be the Initiator

"And when Jesus came to the place, He looked up and saw him, and said to him, 'Zacchaeus, make haste and come down, for today I must stay at your house'" (Luke 19:5).

In Luke 19:1-10, we read of the only instance in the four Gospels where Jesus invited Himself over to someone's home. Employed as an IRS agent, Zaccheus was a wealthy man yet regarded as a notorious sinner by the religious elite and despised by the common people. Let's just say he was not a much sought-after friend. But Jesus saw him up in that tree and did what nobody else would do…… He initiated a relationship with him. Marginalized and displaced by his world, Zacchaeus was ready to meet Jesus. And Jesus was ready to meet with him.

You never know who in your circle of influence is ready to meet Jesus. You never know who in your community is waiting for someone to reach out, to call, to ask how you can pray for them, or be invited over for a cup of coffee. Jesus is the great initiator, showing us what can happen when we go outside our comfort zone and connect with the lonely ones among us. We can summarize the Zacchaeus story in four words: Do not wait – initiate!

As you prayerfully lean into Jesus and His Word, He will put someone on your heart. Don't dismiss it – pray and ask: What would you have me do, Lord? You never know. It could be a sycamore tree moment waiting to happen! Hearts all around us are prepared and ready for Jesus, and to see Jesus, they just need to be asked. So if you are longing for friends, be one. Initiate like He did for you. *"For God so loved the world He gave His only Son….."*

Flourishing Friendships: Encouragement

"But continually encourage one another every day, as long as it is called 'Today'...." (Hebrews 3:13).

Life is hard. Seems discouragement is constantly crouching at the door of our hearts, waiting for just the right opportunity to attack. As if human and circumstantial adversity weren't enough, the enemy of our soul also attacks us from within, barraging us with his fiery arrows of accusations and condemnation. All with the intended end game of getting us to quit. To quit the race. To quit the fight. To wave the white flag of life and say, "No mas."

And this is why we need each other. We need community, like Moses needed Aaron and Hur to hold up his arms in the battle against the Amalekites (Exodus 17). For the Lone Rangers in the Christian life do not last long. They are like the isolated antelopes who become separated from the herd, for your *"adversary the devil walks about like a roaring lion, seeking whom he may devour"* (1 Peter 5:8).

The Bible teaches us to encourage – to deposit courage into each other – to point each other to hope and confidence in the Lord. An encourager infuses the atmosphere with life and hope, pointing others to look up to God and His life-giving promises. The good news is we don't have to wait for others to encourage us; we can water others, give a blessing, and recognize we reap what we sow. If you are feeling a bit low in your encouragement tank today, prayerfully look around and see who you can nourish. As you pour biblical encouragement into someone else, they, in turn, will be strengthened, enabling them to do the same for others.

Here, then, is the path for our own resiliency to finish the race. To finish the fight. As Paul encourages us in Romans 15:

"Let each of us please his neighbor for his good, to build him up. For whatever was written in former days was written for our instruction, that through endurance and through the encouragement of the Scriptures we might have hope. May the God of endurance and encouragement grant you to live in such harmony with one another, in accord with Christ Jesus. Therefore welcome one another as Christ has welcomed you, for the glory of God."

Flourishing Friendships: Cultivating an Unoffendable Heart

"Then He said to His disciples, "It is impossible that no offenses should come…." (Luke 17:1).

Haven't we all experienced treatment from others we've deemed worthy of a justifiable offense in response? In fact, some of the greatest pain inflicted on us has probably come from within the Christian community. For when we're in close community with others, opportunities for misunderstanding, unfulfilled expectations, and downright sin can wreak havoc on our lives. It's just the way life is. The question is not whether it will ever happen to me but how I will respond when it does. Prayerfully reflect on the following Scriptures as you lean into Jesus (From *Embracing Trust* by Joanna Weaver):

1. **1 Corinthians 13:5** – *What* triggers you? Ask the Lord to help you identify your weak spots.
2. **Psalm 139:23-24** – Ask the Holy Spirit to reveal unresolved issues. *Why* did that trigger me?
3. **Matthew 18:15** – Ask God to help you identify offenses as they happen. Don't let them pile up.
4. **Hebrews 8:12** – By grace, He can help us to choose not to remember. Take painful memories to Jesus.
5. **Proverbs 27:6** – Refuse to be defensive. Be open, listen, and pray. Might there be some truth??
6. **1 Cor. 13:7** – Determine to believe the best about people. Default to *innocent until proven guilty.*
7. **Romans 12:18** – Don't pick up another one's offense: You've been given the ministry of reconciliation!
8. **James 1:19** – Hide God's Word in your heart. Just as Jesus did when tempted.
9. **1 Peter 3:9** – Pray blessings over your enemies. Pray *for* those who have hurt you.

"Love one another. As I have loved you, so you must love one another. By this all men will know that you are my disciples, if you love one another" (John 13:34-35).

Hide and Seek

"But Jesus often withdrew to lonely places and prayed" (Luke 5:16).

In our digitized age, when just about anyone can claim hundreds if not thousands of "friends," how ironic we find ourselves suffering from an epidemic of loneliness. A 2021 American Perspective Survey showed Americans report fewer close friendships than ever before. And survey data from 2019 showed 58% of Americans often felt like no one in their life knew them well. However, the problem is not limited to the United States. In 2018, UK Prime Minister Theresa May created a new cabinet position titled *Minister of Loneliness,* something Japan followed suit with in 2021. Two countries hoping they can stem the tide of societal isolation and increased suicide rates.

Recently, a single friend expressed to us their struggle with loneliness. To flee from his fear of being alone, this person realized he had busied himself with many activities and distractions over time—some good, others not so much. And yet, with hindsight, he concluded all his activity was primarily done because of a deep and inherent fear of loneliness brought on by his four walls of silence.

In the rhythm of His busy life, Jesus often withdrew to solitary and deserted places to be alone. To seek His Father. Alone, and yet not, He found companionship and communion in these hidden places. How counterintuitive it is to go *towards* solitary places and not away from them as one strategy in our fight against loneliness. Conventional wisdom says a steady stream of people, sound, and sight (real or virtual) will keep our loneliness at bay. And it will. For a while. Until there is silence, and we find ourselves lonely once again. The good news as disciples and followers of Christ is we have a Constant Companion who will never leave us or forsake us. For us, we have a presence in our solitary and deserted places. The person of Jesus Christ. Something no *Minister of Loneliness* will ever be able to provide. As John Mark Comer stated in his book *Practicing the Way*:

> "…..find your secret place. Go there as often as you can. Prioritize it. Fall in love with it, with God. Without quiet prayer, your life with God will wither; with it, you will come alive to the greatest joy of life: a familiar friendship with Jesus."

A Greater War

"Therefore put to death your members which are on the earth: fornication, uncleanness, passion, evil desire, and covetousness, which is idolatry. But above all…. put on love, which is the bond of perfection" (Colossians 3:5, 14).

In the Old Testament, we read many times where God told Israel, through His servant Joshua, to drive out the wicked inhabitants of Canaan and destroy their idols before settling in the Promised Land. Chosen as His instrument of justice, He used Israel through physical warfare to eradicate wickedness and remove every trace of sin from the land. For they were a holy people living in the presence of a Holy God, *"Therefore do not defile the land which you inhabit, in the midst of which I dwell; for I the Lord dwell among the children of Israel"* (Numbers 35:34). Repeatedly He warned them if they did not obey Him in this, the nations would later become a source of significant irritation leading them to compromise and corruption. Israel would go to war against the people of the land, but they did not fully obey their Commanding General, and as we know, His warnings came to pass.

As a follower of Christ, you also have been called to war. You who are now *"a holy nation"* (1 Peter 2:9). A dwelling place for the Living God, a *"temple of the Holy Spirit"* (1 Corinthians 6:19). In the person of Jesus Christ, the types and shadows of the Old Testament have been fulfilled in the New. You fight, not with the weapons of this world, but with spiritual weapons *"mighty in God for pulling down strongholds"* (1 Corinthians 10:4). You fight a greater war against sin and the devil. Not people. A battleground fought in the realm of the soul, not land. In this fight, unlike the Israelites, do not hesitate to kill all sin living in you. God has empowered and enabled you to do so through His Word and His Spirit, giving you *"the victory through our Lord Jesus Christ"* (1 Corinthians 15:57).

From the song *Take Shelter* by Keith and Kristyn Getty:

> *When a greater war had torn apart my soul*
> *And the iron hold of sin would not let go*
> *All of heaven stormed the darkness*
> *In the power of the cross*
> *I'm freed beneath the banner of His love*

Round Up

"And God is able to make all grace abound toward you, that you, always having all sufficiency in all things, may have an abundance for every good work" (2 Corinthians 9:8).

Usain Bolt is generally regarded as the greatest sprinter of all time, once clocked at 27.33 miles per hour. He holds the world record in the 100-meter and 200-meter dashes and has garnered eight gold medals across three separate Summer Olympic Games. And yet, despite all these incredible accomplishments and his blazing speed, I suspect that's not how it all began for Usain. In fact, at one point, I believe you and I were just as fast as Usain, for one must crawl before one can walk or even run.

Throughout Scripture, we are exhorted to be generous. *"Good will come to those who are generous and lend freely, who conduct their affairs with justice"* (Psalm 112:5). *"You will be enriched in every way to be generous in every way, which through us will produce thanksgiving to God"* (2 Corinthians 9:11). The generous soul is indeed blessed, and a generous spirit blesses others. But where do you start when generosity is not your natural inclination or default? When a scarcity mindset and a spirit of lack rule your soul and determine your financial decisions? It may be time to take a baby step.

My happy place is our local hardware store. Whenever I checkout there, they always ask me if I'd like to *"round up"* for some local charity. What a small yet significant way we might begin the process of becoming more generous. When you provide a tip at a restaurant, round up. When you pay someone back, round up. When you contribute to a gift, round up. We all must start somewhere, and when we do, we will discover our generosity muscles getting stronger, enabling us to move from crawling to walking to running. *"For God loves a cheerful giver"* (2 Corinthians 9:7).

Game Day

"You have come to Mount Zion and to the city of the living God, the heavenly Jerusalem, to an innumerable company of angels and church of the firstborn who are registered in heaven, to God the Judge of all….to Jesus, the Mediator of the new covenant" (Hebrews 12:22-24).

No Olympic athlete ever woke up on the day of their event, having never practiced. Quite the opposite. To prepare for that brief moment, an Olympic athlete trained intensely for many years, having sacrificed sleep, free time, and diet to win the prize. No NFL football team ever spent a leisurely week on the beach leading up to Sunday's game. Instead, they studied game film, lifted weights, ran plays, worked out, and diligently reviewed the game plan for victory. And no successful employee just showed up on the day of a big board presentation without putting a lot of time, thought, and energy into their preparation.

What is the epicenter of your week? When is your game day? For the believer, our game day is church, for we are *"a chosen generation, a royal priesthood, a holy nation, His own special people, that you may proclaim the praises of Him who called you out of darkness into His marvelous light; who once were not a people but are now the people of God, who had not obtained mercy but now have obtained mercy"* (2 Peter 2:9-10).

When we gather together on Sunday morning, two fundamental and glorious things happen. We are not only getting prepared for heaven as we gather with our brothers and sisters in Christ, but we are also actually *joining* heaven, for when we come together corporately, we are coming *"to Mount Zion and to the city of the living God, the heavenly Jerusalem."* This is why the writer of Hebrews says earlier not to forsake *"the assembling of ourselves together as is the manner of some, but exhorting one another, and so much the more as you see the Day approaching"* (Hebrews 10:25).

Let's not stroll into church on Sunday unprepared. God has graciously given us Monday through Saturday to practice and get ready, to spend time throughout the week in His Word, prayer, praise, and fellowship. He is worthy of our readiness, so we might joyfully *"Enter into His gates with thanksgiving, and into His courts with praise. Be thankful to Him, and bless His name"* (Psalm 100:4).

Christ our Curse

"Christ has redeemed us from the curse of the law, having become a curse for us (for it is written, 'Cursed is everyone who hangs on a tree'), that the blessing of Abraham might come upon the Gentiles in Christ Jesus, that we might receive the promise of the Spirit through faith" (Galatians 3:13-14).

I recently read in Deuteronomy 28 the blessings and curses of the covenant God made with the children of Israel as they were about to enter the promised land. Fourteen verses are devoted to the blessings, and fifty-four to the curses. As I read through this chapter, I couldn't help but be so thankful for Jesus, His finished work, and the great exchange He accomplished on the cross. For those in Christ, there is no curse, for He became cursed for us. Jesus absorbed all the curses of Deuteronomy 28:15-68 on the cross for you and me: The fury of God's wrath and His intense anger. While it was a component of the Old Covenant, to be struck *"with madness, blindness, and confusion of heart"* (Deuteronomy 28:28), it will not occur to us under the New, for Christ was struck in our place. In Jesus, we Gentiles are the recipients of the blessings of Abraham, and it's all because of Jesus Christ and what He accomplished on the tree. Which doesn't mean life will be easy. Just ask Paul:

"From the Jews five times I received forty stripes minus one. Three times I was beaten with rods; once I was stoned; three times I was shipwrecked; a night and a day I have been in the deep;....in weariness and toil, in sleeplessness often, in hunger and thirst, in fastings often, in the cold and nakedness..." (2 Corinthians 11:24-25, 27).

Life was no picnic for him. And yet, living under the blessings of Abraham, Paul could conclude, in this same letter, that these were but mere *"...light and momentary afflictions..."* (2 Corinthians 4:17). This is the power of the cross, and the power of Christ living in us (Galatians 2:20). Blessed and set free from the curse of the law by the blood of Jesus, *"There is therefore now no condemnation to those who are in Christ Jesus, who do not walk according to the flesh, but according to the Spirit"* (Romans 8:1).

From the hymn *I Will Sing of My Redeemer:*

I will sing of my Redeemer and His wondrous love to me;
On the cruel cross He suffered, from the curse to set me free.
Sing, O sing of my Redeemer, with His blood he purchased me;
On the cross He sealed my pardon, paid the debt and made me free.

I Believe in the Name of Jesus: Trust

"Then Jesus lifted up His eyes, and seeing a great multitude coming toward Him, He said to Philip, 'Where shall we buy bread, that these may eat?' Philip answered Him, 'Two hundred denarii worth of bread is not sufficient for them, that every one of them may have a little'" (John 6:5, 7).

Jesus' question to Philip must have sounded a little preposterous to him. For the passage says there were five thousand *men* (v. 10), which did not include the women and children accompanying them. So when Philip responded with the craziest number he could come up with in the moment (200 denarii being about seven months of wages), it still fell incredibly short. Jesus, wanting to provide everyone with a banquet, had stumped His disciples. What were they going to do? On top of a mountain, in the wilderness, with no Costco in sight and poor Wi-Fi reception for DoorDash, the team was certainly in a profound dilemma.

Jesus' question of Philip was really all about his faith. The disciples had lived in the presence of Jesus and had seen Him perform every kind of creative miracle: turning water into wine, healing lepers, and even raising the dead. Witnessing miracles was nothing new to them. But at that moment, with more than ten thousand people needing to eat, they were confronted with a problem totally different from anything they had faced before. Their line of sight was controlling their level of faith. After seeing Jesus perform so many miracles, we expect the disciples to immediately turn to Him and say, "Lord, we trust you; You can do anything." But the disciples did not count on the Lord to be the solution.

And many times, neither do we. Faced with a problem, a conundrum, or a dilemma needing a solution, we immediately rack our brains to come up with the fix. How prone we are to lean on our own understanding rather than trust in the Lord for that solution. This is why God will bring impossible circumstances into our lives, forcing us to turn to Him rather than our typical human default. Like feeding thousands of people with five loaves and two fish. Like Paul and his companions, who *"had the sentence of death in ourselves that we should not trust in ourselves but in God who raises the dead"* (2 Corinthians 1:9).

I Believe in the Name of Jesus: When to be Grateful

"Then Jesus said, 'Make the people sit down.' Now there was much grass in the place. So the men sat down, in number about five thousand. And Jesus took the loaves, and when He had given thanks he distributed them to the disciples, and the disciples to those sitting down; and likewise of the fish, as much as they wanted" (John 6:10-11).

Holding the small amount of food brought by the young lad, Jesus gave thanks. *Before* there was a visible answer. Expressing gratitude for the provision *before* there was enough to feed the multitudes. Here, Jesus provides a blueprint for us to give thanks before seeing our needs fully met. Jesus thanked the One He knew to be the Source, for every good and perfect gift comes from above. In doing this, He lived out the will of His Heavenly Father here on earth. For with Jesus, everything He did was intentional and deliberate, for He said, *"My food is to do the will of Him who sent Me, and to finish His work"* (John 4:34).

And here we also see Jesus revealing Himself as the Lord of multiplication. His arm is not too short to save, for with God, all things are possible. The practical lesson for us is clear: Whenever there is a need, give all we have to Jesus and trust Him for the rest. He can take our meager resources and multiply them for His purposes. For He *"is able to do exceedingly abundantly above all that we ask or think,"* so let us not limit the Holy One of Israel. In the end, the multitude had *"as much as they wanted,* and *"were filled,"* while the disciples *"filled twelve baskets"* with the leftovers. So bring what you have and give Him thanks in advance for what He alone can do.

From the hymn *Thanks to God!*:

Thanks, O God for boundless mercy from Thy gracious throne above;
Thanks for every need provided from the fullness of Thy love.
Thanks for daily toil and labor and for rest when shadows fall;
Thanks for love of friend and neighbor, and Thy goodness unto all.

Thanks for thorns as well as roses, thanks for weakness and for health;
Thanks for clouds as well as sunshine, thanks for poverty and wealth.
Thanks for pain as well as pleasure – all Thou sendest day by day;
And Thy Word, our dearest treasure, shedding light upon our way.

I Believe in the Name of Jesus: Life in Christ

"For the bread of God is He who comes down from heaven and gives life to the world. Then they said to Him, 'Lord, give us this bread always.' And Jesus said to them, 'I am the bread of life. He who comes to Me shall never hunger, and he who believes in Me shall never thirst'" (John 6:33-35).

As you read John 6, you will see a fascinating progression regarding Jesus and His followers. At the beginning, *"a great multitude followed Him"* (v. 2), and towards the end, many of His disciples *"walked with Him no more" (v.* 66). What happened? Why did the crowds so quickly unfollow Him?

Jesus knew the people sought Him *"because you ate of the loaves and were filled" (v. 26).* They didn't want Him; they wanted what He could do for them. A cosmic Santa Claus or slot machine. Wanting to work and earn their way to God so they could get more of that delicious bread He provided the other day, they asked Him, *"What shall we do, that we may work the works of God?" (v. 29).* For in their quest to work, their genuine desire was *"Lord, give us this bread always" (v. 34).* They wanted the typical human transaction: We do this, then you do that. That was until Jesus put a big damper on the party, *"I am the Living Bread which came down from heaven. If anyone eats of this bread, he will live forever; and the bread that I shall give is My own flesh, which I shall give for the life of the world" (v. 51).* Insert arguing, quarreling, complaining, and a mass exodus of followers here.

If we want to grow, if we want our eyes to be open, if we want our roots to go down deep into the fertile soil of life with Jesus, we have to eat of the Living Bread… the living and active Word of God. For it points us to the Word who became flesh. The Scriptures point us to Jesus, our Source of true sustenance and nourishment (John 5:39-40). Even He said to the devil, *"It is written, 'Man shall not live by bread alone, but by every word that proceeds from the mouth of God'"* (Matthew 4:4). So, like the Israelites who had to collect their manna daily, let's hunger and thirst for Jesus every day. In doing so, He will be faithful to give us Himself, our Daily Bread.

Follow the Leader

*"And He is the head of the body, the church, who is the beginning,
the firstborn from the dead, that in all things He may have
the preeminence" (Colossians 1:18).*

I am no physician, but as I understand the human body, the brain is like a computer controlling all the body's functions, with the central nervous system constantly relaying messages back and forth from the brain to the other members of the body. In a healthy body, these members comply with the brain's instructions. When the brain says to open the door, the hand and other body parts comply. We don't see the members rebelling, staging a mutiny, or forming a class action lawsuit against the brain in a healthy body. In fact, with messages from the brain traveling approximately 393 feet/second, the brain and body are constantly dancing in this beautiful, invisible choreography of initiation and response.

In the same way, and beyond mere metaphor, this is how the body of Christ operates. He is the head, and we are His members. Christ is present on the earth in and through us. As Head, Christ leads and instructs us, not vice versa. Now, *how* He leads may not always conform to our conventional wisdom, for He put the choir out in front of the army as Judah went to battle (2 Chronicles 20:21), and He told his people to march and shout to bring down the walls of Jericho (Joshua 5:3-5). That's not conventional.

What stands in the way of this beautiful dance is primarily our own will. "No, Lord (oxymoron, BTW), I won't do that." "No, Lord, that's inconvenient." "No, Lord, that's outside my comfort zone." "No, Lord, that doesn't make any sense." These are the responses of an unhealthy body. And so, like Jesus, we need to go to our Garden of Gethsemane daily. *"Father, if it is Your will, take this cup away from Me; nevertheless, not My will, but Yours, be done"* (Luke 22:42), for *"Not everyone who says to Me, 'Lord, Lord,' shall enter the kingdom of heaven, but he who does the will of My Father in heaven"* (Matthew 7:21).

From the hymn *Trust and Obey:*

*Trust and obey
For there's no other way
To be happy in Jesus,
But to trust and obey.*

Freeze Frame

"Who are you to judge another's servant? To his own master he stands or falls. Indeed, he will be made to stand, for God is able to make him stand" (Romans 14:4).

For those of you who are not in the least bit interested in sports, please humor me as I attempt to use a sports metaphor and apply it to life. Biased as a lover of competition, I firmly believe any game (or *match* for you futbol fans) is a microcosm of life. You have a start, a middle, and an end. You have the thrill of victory and the agony of defeat. You have offense and defense. You have easy games and hard games. You have ease of schedule, and you have adversity of schedule. You have teammates and opponents. Superstars and benchwarmers. Fans and haters. Sure sounds like life to me!

One thing about a sporting event is it is always dynamic. Never static. If I take a snapshot in time, say with 8 minutes to go in the second quarter, that in no way ensures I have an accurate read on how the game will end. In fact, any conclusions I draw at that moment in time about the ending will be highly flawed. If it's so glaringly apparent in sports we shouldn't draw such conclusions; why don't we possess this same level of clarity with the people we bump into throughout life?

People, families, organizations, and churches change over the course of time. And so do you. If I were to take a picture of your 2010 self, it would probably be much different than your current self. When we cling to a snapshot in time of another person or group (whether a week or a decade ago), we've judged them, sentenced them, and placed them in the prison of our mind, where they remain forever frozen in solitary confinement. This is the outcome of holding onto a past offense and/or believing your historical snapshot of another human is still highly accurate today.

Instead, how about we give others the benefit of the doubt? Let's glorify God by assuming He *"is able to make him [or her] stand."* He is able! One of the best principles I've found in life when interacting with others is to default to *innocent until proven guilty*. With the passage of time, let's assume the best about people rather than the worst. Let's assume they've changed and changed for the better. For Jesus taught us, *"Blessed are the merciful, for they shall obtain mercy"* (Matthew 5:7). And because *"Mercy triumphs over judgment"* (James 2:13), in the absence of information, let's be *"looking unto Jesus, the author and <u>finisher</u> of our faith"* (Hebrews 12:2). Our faith and theirs. The game isn't over yet.

Return on Investment

"... for a little while, if need be, you have been grieved by various trials, that the genuineness of your faith, being much more precious than gold... "
(1 Peter 1-6-7).

As I write this, the value of gold is skyrocketing. From an investment and hindsight perspective, it may have been wise to purchase some of it a few months back. In fact, about a year ago, Costco started selling 24-carat gold bars, creating quite a frenzy with its customers. Regularly running out of stock, analysts estimate Costco is currently selling approximately $200 million a month in gold bars.

Thought experiment: Say I back a dump truck into your driveway. In it is a full payload of gold bars. I then knock on your door, have you come out, and make you an offer. You can have all the gold in the dump truck, or you can have greater faith—say, Hebrews 11 kind of faith. Which would you choose? While hypothetical, I daresay that might be a tough decision for many of us. Myself included. But it does beg the question: What do we value the most? For Jesus said, *"... where your treasure is, there your heart will be also"* (Matthew 6:21).

While Jesus spoke of requiring just *"faith as a mustard seed"* (Matthew 17:20), He also marveled when He encountered a centurion of great faith (Matthew 8:10) and gently rebuked Peter with *"O you of little faith... "* (Matthew 14:31). So, it seems our level of faith can develop and enlarge... from little to great. And, it seems, faith is extremely valuable in God's eyes. Otherwise, why Hebrews 11? Specially Hebrews 11:6, *"But without faith it is impossible to please Him, for He who comes to God must believe that He is, and that He is a rewarder of those who diligently seek Him."* Faith in Him, whether receiving a loved one back from the dead (Hebrews 11:35) or being sawn in two (11:37). Our Father wants us to trust Him, irrespective of circumstances.

The bedrock of all healthy relationships, faith says you believe Him and take Him at His Word. As we see God's faithfulness time and time again over the years, our trust in Him grows. We find Him dependable, always keeping His Word, and always worthy of our trust. And when we have such faith in Him, we experience His pleasure, for this is what He values so highly. So, let's align our value system with His and invest wisely. Christ alone is our Supreme Treasure. Only He can satisfy and fill our longing hearts.

I Am the Light of the World

"Then Jesus spoke to them again, saying, 'I am the light of the world. He who follows Me shall not walk in darkness, but have the light of life'"
(John 8:12).

The immediate context of the above verse is the story of the woman caught in adultery (John 8:1-11). Picture the scene in your mind: Jesus is sitting in the Temple, teaching the people. The Pharisees come barging in with a woman caught in the very act of adultery. Right away, Jesus is tipped off that something is amiss because they only bring in one of the two guilty parties. The law clearly required both to be put to death (Leviticus 20:10). The Pharisees, expecting Jesus to join them in their hypocritical stoning of the condemned and humiliated woman, instead stooped. *"But Jesus bent down and wrote on the ground with His finger"* (v. 6). Like their hard hearts; He bent down to write on the hard ground of the temple with His finger, the very finger of God. Instead of raising Himself in judgment, the King of Kings stooped.

This is what grace does. It bends down to meet us. Grace meets us at our point of need through the Person of Jesus Christ. In all of His power and provision. Having dispersed the guilty Pharisaical mob by having them face their own sin, Jesus then says, *"Woman, where are those accusers of yours? Has no one condemned you?"* (v. 10). She answers, *"No one, Lord"* (v. 11). Gone were the voices of accusation and condemnation. The ones who claimed to know the law of God, but did not know the God of the law. But the woman did, and from Him she would receive her freedom, for His kindness leads us to repentance.

And while Jesus did not condemn her for her sin, He did not condone it either. *"Go and sin no more"* (v. 11). Do you think after this experience the woman continued in her sin? I suspect not. Jesus changed her life that day. Just as He did with the woman at the well (John 4), Jesus opened her eyes to the very One who was the Truth, setting her free to walk in His light and in darkness no longer. The very same plan Jesus has for you and me.

Where are you looking?

"And as Moses lifted up the serpent in the wilderness, even so must the Son of Man be lifted up, that whoever believes in Him should not perish but have eternal life" (John 3:14-15).

In the book of Luke, we are presented with two individuals who had much in common but experienced two very diverse outcomes in their encounters with Jesus. While the rich young ruler (18:18-23) and Zacchaeus (19:1-10) both possessed authority and wealth, one walked away from Jesus with sorrow, while the other *"received Him joyfully"* (19:6). Why was that?

To answer that question, we must first understand what Jesus was alluding to in the above passage in John. In the Old Testament (Numbers 21:4-9), we learn about the Israelites complaining yet again and how *"the Lord sent fiery serpents among the people, and they bit the people, and many of the people died"* (21:6). God's remedy? Have Moses put a bronze serpent on a pole and lift it up, *"and it shall be that everyone who is bitten when he looks at it, shall live"* (21:8). Jesus was saying, like the bronze serpent, look to Me, and you too will be saved. Not from fiery serpents but from the poison of sin.

And this is why these two men went in very opposite directions. The rich young ruler wanted the best of both worlds. He wanted to keep his earthly wealth, he wanted to *do* something, and he wanted eternal life. But He didn't want Jesus. On the other hand, Zacchaeus just wanted to look upon Jesus, *"And he sought to see who Jesus was"* (19:3). One wanted to work for eternal life, while the other just wanted to look at Him. One wanted to keep his earthly treasure (18:23), while the other was willing to give it all away (19:8).

Where are you looking today? Are you willing to give up whatever you must to see more of Christ? Are you looking to His hand for what He can do for you, or to His face, where love will transform you from the inside out? *"For it is God who commanded light to shine out of darkness, who has shone in our hearts to give the light of the knowledge of the glory of God in the face of Jesus Christ"* (2 Corinthians 4:6). Unlike the anonymous rich young ruler, look to the face of Christ, and He too will call you by name.

The Real Deal

"But solid is for the mature, who by constant use have trained themselves to distinguish good from evil" (Hebrews 5:14).

When I was a new believer, I asked a pastor about studying the prominent cults of the day. He gave some sage advice I have not forgotten decades later. He pointed me to the banking industry, where employees are trained to distinguish genuine money from counterfeit. He said, "They don't learn to spot counterfeit bills by studying the counterfeit; they study the genuine to identify what is not. Don't study the cults. Read and study your Bible instead." The famous revivalist preacher of long ago, George Whitefield, said:

"If we once get above our Bibles and cease making the written Word of God our sole rule both to faith and practice, we shall soon lie open to all manner of delusion."

Whether or not we are in the final days before Christ returns remains to be seen. What we do know to be true is we are living in the last days, *"God, who at various times and in various ways spoke in time past to the fathers, by the prophets, has in these last days spoken to us by His Son"* (Hebrews 1:1-2). In these last days, we are going up against Satan, who *"masquerades as an angel of light"* (2 Corinthians 11:4), the very one who will bring......

"... all power, signs, and lying wonders, and with all unrighteous deception among those who perish, because they did not receive the love of the truth, that they might be saved. And for this reason God will send them strong delusion" (Thessalonians 2:9-11).

Deception. Delusion. This is the world in which we live. We're being inundated with half-truths spoken as full-truths. These are nothing more than non-truths. God's antidote? His written Word. And not just dabbling in it: *"who by constant use."* It's both quality *and* quantity. A few minutes in His Word does not counterbalance hours and hours of deception and delusion. So let's be disciples, diligently studying the Scriptures, for they point us to the One who is *"the Way, the Truth, and the Life"* (John 14:6).

The Real Deal (Part 2)

"But solid is for the mature, who by constant use have trained themselves to distinguish good from evil" (Hebrews 5:14).

The devil typically does not knock on your door and say, "Hello, my name is Satan. As you can see, I'm red and have pointy ears; this is my pitchfork. I am here to take you with me to hell." Instead, he employs something much more sinister, for he is well aware of what he is engaged in. He is in a war. And because of that, Satan is diabolically skilled in the art and science of deception.

To defeat an enemy in war, you must excel in deception. In a war, tanks need to look like trees, ships need to look like the ocean, planes need to be invisible, and military personnel need to appear as shrubs and plants. Cold wars are no different. The deception just finds itself in different forms. In a cold war, espionage is employed to obtain military secrets. This is done by using spies, secret agents, and monitoring devices. A friend is really your enemy, allies are not on your side, and that lamp on the table is listening to everything being said. Whether hot or cold, all wars are won by how well you can deceive and delude the other side.

For us to win our spiritual war, at least two things must occur. First and foremost, we must realize we are indeed in a war. I'm afraid far too many believers think we live in a time of peace when nothing could be further from the truth. Rather than wearing spiritual shorts and flip-flops into our daily battlefield, every day we must wear the whole armor of God, lifting up the shield of faith and wielding the sword of the Spirit, which is the Word of God (Ephesians 6:10-18). And second, we must *"distinguish good from evil."* Emphasis on *distinguishing*. Meaning, it will not always be obvious what is good and what is evil.

To fight and partake in Christ's victory, we must embrace what He has provided to live in victory and defeat our deceptive enemy. We must devour His Word, be empowered by His Holy Spirit in prayer, and remain actively integrated with His Bride, the Church. These are the weapons our Commander has outfitted us with. Having these, we have the power to *"reign in life"* (Romans 5:17) and *"be more than conquerors through Him who loved us"* (Romans 8:37).

Right-Side-Up

"But now having been set free from sin, and having become slaves of God, you have your fruit to holiness, and the end, everlasting life" (Romans 6:22).

The Bible is full of paradoxes. Not only does the Word redefine reality for believers, it also causes us to rethink our word associations. For instance, do you connotate freedom with the word *slavery*? I would venture to say no. And yet, *"It is for freedom that Christ has set us free"* (Galatians 5:1). In Christ, as slaves of God, we have been set free. This is just one example of the counterintuitive worldview brought by Christ. When we come to Jesus, our human paradigms, frameworks, and terms get turned upside down. Or perhaps more accurately, in Christ, everything gets turned right-side-up. In what other ways has Christ redeemed us and our minds?

"Return to the stronghold, you prisoners of hope. Even today I declare that I will restore double to you" (Zechariah 9:12). Prisoners of hope. Don't we all want to be cast and confined into that prison? Jesus has incarcerated us to a perpetual hope—a life sentence without eligibility for parole. Hallelujah, sign me up! *"Blessed be the God and Father of our Lord Jesus Christ, who according to His abundant mercy has begotten us again to a living hope... "* (1 Peter 1:3).

"Do they not go astray who devise evil? But mercy and truth belong to those who devise good" (Proverbs 14:22). The word *devise* has been hijacked to generally connotate plans to do evil. What only the bad guys like Hitler and Darth Vadar do. To plot something wicked. But imagine a world where we were constantly scheming to do good. Devising good for others with the same level of intensity villains plan to take over the world or rule the galaxies.

"... in a great trial of affliction the abundance of their joy and their deep poverty abounded in the riches of their liberality" (2 Corinthians 8:2). When I hear of those experiencing great trials and deep poverty, I do not immediately associate those same people having abundant joy, great riches, and generous giving. And yet, welcome to the Macedonian churches. Contrary to human reasoning, their generosity sprang from the joy they experienced in the middle of their hardship and destitution.

Enslaved for freedom. Imprisoned for hope. Devising good for others. Joy and generosity springing from trial and poverty. The paradoxical life is now the right-side-up life we have in Jesus.

Curate and Flourish: We Become What We Behold

"We all, with unveiled face, beholding the glory of the Lord, are being transformed into the same image from one degree of glory to another. For this comes from the Lord who is the Spirit" (2 Corinthians 3:18).

In other words, Paul is saying we are being transformed into His likeness by looking intently at who He is. As we behold Christ, we become like Christ. We become what we behold. Whatever we focus on is the very thing we are being transformed into. What we focus on, we empower in our lives. If we focus on our fears, anxiety, and stress, we become fearful, anxious, and stressed out. What is dominating your focus these days? What are you beholding? The enemy of your soul wants to get our minds off God's sufficiency and onto ourselves instead – our fear, our anxiety, our inadequacy. So, where do we begin this transformational process?

We begin with our thoughts, for every action is rooted in the thought that produced it. Negative thoughts begat negative actions. The starting line is our mind: *"And do not be conformed to this world, but be transformed by the renewing of your mind, that you may prove what is that good, and acceptable, and perfect will of God"* (Romans 12:2). If all our thinking has brought us to a place we do not like, we need to exchange our thinking for one of God's thoughts. We need to exchange those negative thoughts for thoughts of who we are in Christ and the promises He's given to us in His Word.

For example, perhaps you are in a situation right now, and you find yourself saying, "This is so hard," or "I'm so stressed out," or "I'm so anxious about our money." Remember, what you focus on, you empower. The Bible reveals to us over and over again there is no stress or anxiety in Jesus. Jesus is the Prince of Peace. This is what He brings to those who are His. Our identity and position in Him challenge our circumstances. God speaks to us through His Word. And when God speaks to us, He wants to get us to see, know, and understand things from His perspective – this is called the renewing of the mind. This is why God tells us in His Word to *"bring every thought into captivity to the obedience of Christ"* (2 Corinthians 10:5). God's best for us is to have our perception, thinking, and mindset align with His Word and His view of us and our circumstances.

So let us look away, look up to Jesus, and *"… behold the beauty of the Lord"* (Psalm 27:4).

Curate and Flourish:
The Enormity of Small Choices

"Do not be deceived, God is not mocked; for whatever a man sows, that he will also reap" (Galatians 6:7).

Did you know that if a pilot leaving LAX adjusts the heading to just 3.5% south, the plane will land in Washington, D.C., and not New York? Such a slight change would not even be noticed at takeoff – the nose of the plane moves just a few feet – but when magnified across the entire United States, the plane lands over two hundred and twenty miles to the south.

What is true of flight is also true of our personal lives. A slight change in our daily habits can guide us to a vastly different destination. In our desire for life's big defining moments or breakthroughs, we underestimate the value of making small improvements each day. Making daily improvements by just 1% (far less than 3.5%!) can be much more meaningful over time than the breakthrough, for your daily habits act like compound interest. What would a daily 1% improvement look like compounded over the course of a lifetime?

For instance, one practical step might be to begin keeping a thankfulness journal. Start each day by reflecting on the day before, writing down three things to thank and praise God for. Such a small thing, yet so significant in drawing closer to God: *"It is good to give thanks to the Lord, and to sing praises to Your name, O Most High; to declare your lovingkindness in the morning, and Your faithfulness every night" (*Psalm 92:1). It may not sound like a big deal, but over time the compounding nature of a grateful life will produce a bountiful, eternal crop. And don't we all want our planes to land in the beautiful city of gratitude?

Choosing 1% better or 1% worse may seem insignificant now, but ultimately, those choices will be the difference between who you are and who you could be. This is the Biblical principle of sowing and reaping. Begin sowing the eternal seeds now, cultivating an intentional life. One day, one moment at a time. It's all about trajectory. All important things come from small beginnings. God is in the business of watering seeds sown in the soil of His Word, so *"Do not despise the day of small beginnings"* (Zechariah 4:10). There will be many days to begin again, but a life marked with beginning will gradually grow into a life marked by doing.

Curate and Flourish: He Had to Pass Through Samaria

"He left Judea and departed again for Galilee. And He had to pass through Samaria. So He came to a town of Samaria called Sychar, near the field that Jacob had given to his son Joseph. Jacob's well was there; so Jesus, wearied as he was from His journey, was sitting beside the well. It was about the sixth hour [noon]" (John 4:3-6).

Jesus could have taken three possible routes on His way back to Galilee: Along the coast, across the Jordan, or straight up the middle through Samaria. Most Jews avoided Samaria because of the deep-seated hatred between them and the Samaritans. The Samaritans were a mixed race of part Jew and part Gentile, having grown out of the Assyrian captivity of the ten northern tribes. The Jews rejected them because they could not prove their genealogy. They had established their own temple and religious services on Mt. Gerazim, which only helped fan the flames of prejudice.

Jesus *"had to pass through Samaria"* because there He would meet a woman and lead her into saving faith, the kind of faith that would forever change her and her entire village. Jesus *"had to pass through"* to reveal God loves all people. The Living Word – the Gospel in the flesh – is more powerful than prejudice, bias, racism, and social traditions. It doesn't matter your skin color, gender, background, or religion – Jesus will go out of His way to make clear the Gospel is for all people. Like the nameless woman in our story, Jesus will always walk and become wearied just for the one.

Do you have a Samaria? Who is in your Samaria? Is there someone in your neighborhood, your office, your extended family, your church, your child's school – is there a prompting in your heart to go to your Samaria? To make time to be with someone who perhaps thinks of you as the enemy? Jesus *had* to go through Samaria to reach the marginalized one with the good news of God's love for her. A despised member of a despised people group, Jesus goes out of His way to show His unconditional love, for she matters to God.

Curate and Flourish: The Gift of Grace

"Jesus said to her, 'Go call your husband, and come here.' The woman answered Him, 'I have no husband.' Jesus said to her, 'You are right in saying, I have no husband; for you have had five husbands, and the one you now have is not your husband. What you have said is true'"
(John 4:16-18).

When Jesus told her to get her husband, He was getting her to admit her sin. Before we can experience saving faith in Jesus, we all must realize our need for a Savior. The good news is only good news because there is first bad news. And that bad news is our sin has separated us from God. *"For all have sinned and fallen short of the glory of God"* (Romans 3:23). We are dead and need resurrection. The free gift of God is our repentance, turning from our wicked ways and turning to Jesus.

While the woman at the well had her mind touched and her emotions stirred, Christ knew she needed her conscience impacted too, which meant dealing with her sin. *"I have no husband"* is the shortest statement she made during their entire conversation – did you notice that? Why? Because now she was realizing her sin. And like most people, she then tries to detour Jesus by discussing the differences between the Jewish and Samaritan religions (John 4:19-20), because it's much more comfortable to discuss religion in general than it is to face your specific life of sin.

"For if by the one man's offense [Adam] death reigned through the one, much more those who receive abundance of grace and of the gift of righteousness will reign in life through the One, Jesus Christ" (Romans 5:17). Here then is the gift of grace: The person of Jesus Christ. Dead, lost, and separated, Jesus came to raise the dead.

From the hymn *Amazing Grace:*

> *Amazing grace how sweet the sound*
> *That saved a wretch like me!*
> *I once was lost but now am found*
> *Was blind but now I see*

Curate and Flourish: Christ Only Always

"So the woman left her waterpot and went away into town and said to the people, 'Come, see a man who told me all that I ever did. Can this be the Christ?' They went out of town and were coming to Him" (John 4:28-30).

As we've mentioned before, what we focus on we empower. Here, we see the Samaritan woman had a complete change of heart. She focused on the truth Jesus revealed and the power of living water He brings to each believer. Leaving her waterpot behind, she ran off to tell everyone in her village about Jesus, for now she had this water inside her. Finally, she was satisfied and complete. Having spent a lifetime trying to fill her God-shaped void with others, she finally found the One the void was originally designed for. Symbolizing her empty heart and unmet needs, she leaves the empty waterpot behind and shares the good news with everyone in her village. She had found her Messiah. And theirs too. Despite racial, gender, and religious barriers, she now knew Jesus, and He was her everything, for He alone is the One who can change the human heart from the inside and cross the barriers of hatred and division with love. For her and for everyone in her village.

Maybe you have an empty waterpot you need to leave behind. Something in your heart or life holding you back—a mindset of unbelief, a lie you've believed, grief over a loss, or a profound hurt or disappointment you've been holding onto. Anger with how things have turned out for your life or how things are going in our world today—anything that leaves us empty and longing. Can we leave it with Jesus today?

From the hymn *Have Thine Own Way, Lord!*:

> *Have Thine own way, Lord. Have Thine own way.*
> *Thou art the Potter, I am the clay.*
> *Mold me and make me after Thy will,*
> *While I am waiting, yielded and still.*

> *Have Thine own way, Lord. Have Thine own way.*
> *Hold o'er my being absolute sway.*
> *Fill with Thy Spirit till all shall see,*
> *Christ only, always, living in me!*

Be Brave (Part 2): Paul and Silas

"About midnight Paul and Silas were praying and singing hymns to God, and the other prisoners were listening to them" (Acts 16:25).

In obedience to his vision (Acts 16:9), Paul goes with Silas to Philippi. He immediately obeys, shares the gospel, builds his first church, and welcomes the first converts in Europe. And amid this extremely fruitful ministry, he and Silas are beaten and cast into the inner dungeon of a Roman prison. As a result of their obedience, the ministry is shut down on the spot. Paul and Silas probably didn't completely understand why their circumstances took a turn for the worse, but they did not allow their lack of understanding to become a wall between them and God. Instead, they deliberately chose to praise God in that prison as an act of their will and faith. They decided to praise God despite their feelings. This is called a sacrifice of praise.

Praising God is not based on feeling. It's based on fact – the fact and truth of Who He is. *"Therefore by Him, let us continually offer the sacrifice of praise to God, that is the fruit of our lips, giving thanks to His name"* (Hebrews 13:15). Praising God when experiencing difficult circumstances shows we trust His Word and love Him. When we are at a low point, we are giving the sacrifice of praise. It shows that we believe God, even when God and His actions do not seem to make sense to our finite minds. Paul knew that praise is faith in action, and praise releases God's power into our lives and circumstances.

Paul and Silas, students of God's Word, quite possibly had these verses on their minds that night: *"He is your praise and He is your God, who has done for you these great and awesome things which your eyes have seen"* (Deuteronomy 10:21). *"You meet him who rejoices and does righteousness, who remembers You in Your ways"* (Isaiah 64:5). *"But You are holy, enthroned in the praises of Israel"* (Psalm 22:3). God inhabits the praises of His people, and when we offer to Him a sacrifice of praise, He shows up in His fullness and power. Sometimes in supernatural acts, but always with His supernatural presence.

Be Brave (Part 2): Chains Fall Off

"Suddenly there was a great earthquake, so that the foundations of the prison were shaken and immediately all the doors were opened and everyone's chains were loosed" (Acts 16:26).

Everyone's chains fell off! What a glorious testimony of what happens in the life of a believer who chooses joy. Our chains fall off as God comes near and He begins to transform our circumstances. Usually figuratively, but sometimes literally. Maybe we won't see a change right away, or perhaps we won't be aware of a shift, but our hearts change, our attitudes change, and our outlook on life changes as our mindset changes. Not only that, but when we worship, we experience the love of God. When we take on something He has ordained – praising Him and choosing joy – it has grace all over it.

As we worship, God clears our minds and brings clarity to His Word. He gives us a fresh revelation of His Son and His love for us. He refreshes, renews, enriches, enlightens, frees, and fills us. He breathes life into the dead and barren areas of our lives. He infuses us with His power and His joy. He will redeem and transform us and our situations. He will fill our empty places and liberate us from bondage, take away our fear and doubt and instead grow our faith and give us peace – all of this as a result of praising Him. He lives in the praises of His people. This is what He brings to where He lives! He meets the one who rejoices.

Charles Spurgeon said:

"God is too good to be unkind and he is too wise to be mistaken. And when we cannot trace His Hand, we must trust His heart. When you are so weak that you cannot do much more than cry, you coin diamonds with both your eyes. The sweetest prayers God ever hears are the groans and sighs of those who have no hope in anything but His love."

Middle

*"Faith does not eliminate questions.
But faith knows where to take them."*

Elisabeth Elliot

Your Story Matters: The Waiting Prophet

"I will stand my watch and set myself on the rampart. And watch to see what He will say to me, and what I will answer when I am corrected"
(Habakkuk 2:1).

The hand dealt Habakkuk was extremely alarming and confusing. The coming invasion of the Chaldeans would be a tool in God's hand for the correction and purification of His people (Hab. 1:12). Deeply troubled by the moral conundrum of God using the Chaldeans in this way, wouldn't that be wrong for God to raise up such a wicked nation? Isn't that tantamount to endorsing evil? *"Your eyes are too pure to look on evil; you cannot tolerate wrong"* (Hab. 1:13). Having no answer, in faith, he commits the problem to God. Here we learn a lot about how to leave a problem with God in faith.

First, he suggests he would enter a watchtower and stand his watch. Watchtowers rose high above fortified cities and enabled a watchman to see an approaching enemy far in the distance. Detached from the everyday activity of life, they are far above the cacophony of street-level noise. Have you ever felt like, amid great difficulty, you have talked something to death but still don't have it resolved or figured out? Then let's learn from his example: Detach and go to God. Get away from all the distractions and position yourself to hear from Him.

Second, expect Him to answer. Habakkuk tells us he will *"watch to see what He will say to me."* Now usually, when someone says something to you, you wait to *hear* it—you don't *see* what they are saying. But Habakkuk is so sure he will hear from God that he confidently declares he will not only listen to it but see it as well. High above in his watchtower, he is watching to see what will happen. In the same way, how do we look for God's answer? How will He speak to us? Directly from Scripture or in alignment with it. When trouble comes, we need to hear from God and recognize His voice. That familiarity comes because we've heard it so frequently from the pages of His Word.

Your Story Matters: Hear... and Then Write it Down

"Then the Lord answered me and said, 'write the vision and make it plain on tablets, that he may run who reads it'" (Habakkuk 2:2).

Hearing the voice of God is our birthright as children of the King. *"My sheep hear My voice, and I know them, and they follow Me"* (John 10:27). *"Behold, I stand at the door and knock. If anyone hears my voice and opens the door, I will come in to him and dine with him, and he with Me"* (Revelation 3:20). And when (not *if*) the Lord speaks to us through His Word, the principle from Habakkuk is clear: Write it down!

One reason to keep a journal or notebook with you in your time in the Word is because we're so good at forgetting. Every day brings shiny new objects, and what shined in the morning is forgotten by the afternoon. So repeatedly in Scripture, and especially with the Israelites, God was and is always instructing His people to remember. *"Do this in remembrance of Me"* (Luke 22:19). Concrete actions help fragile humans to remember. When the Lord speaks to you from His Word, do something tangible to record that historical moment.

Two other takeaways from this verse. First, note this instruction from God is to *"make it plain."* That's how the Lord speaks to us. He doesn't make His guidance, direction, or wisdom complex. Although not always easy, He does make things very clear, and typically, that clarity comes from the Bible. In addition, this transcribed clarity is so we *"may run who reads it."* In other words, the things the Lord tells us are motivational. Our God is the Lord of hope, faith, love, encouragement, and spiritual progress. Including even the rebukes and disciplines of life.

"If people can't see what God is doing, they stumble all over themselves; but when they attend to what He reveals, they are most blessed" (Proverbs 29:18 MSS). Yes, when we see what He is doing and attend to what He reveals, you and I will be the *"most blessed."* This blessed state is a state of spiritual progress, which leads to the progression of His Kingdom. Rather than a self-centered or selfish progression – this is always about the advancement of *His* Kingdom. Your story matters because He is using it in His story, a thread in the tapestry only He can weave.

Your Story Matters: Faith in the Waiting

"For the vision is yet for an appointed time; but at the end it will speak, and it will not lie. Though it tarries, wait for it; because it will surely come, it will not tarry. Behold the proud, his soul is not upright in him; but the just shall live by his faith" (Habakkuk 2:3-4).

Our final step in hearing from God is to wait expectantly for the fulfillment of whatever God has promised or shown you. We must receive vision with patience and faith because it has an appointed time. God promises it will tarry, but He also promises it will be fulfilled. The question for Habakkuk – and us – is *when*. For Habakkuk, it was approximately 20 years before he saw God's Word fulfilled. In our microwave society, this is often our most challenging step. But it is a step nonetheless, so God calls His children to wait patiently and expectantly in faith on Him.

Habakkuk 2:4 is the central verse of this book. It was central then, and it is central now. *"The just* (those who have been justified by the finished work of Jesus Christ on the cross) *shall live by faith."* It's always been about faith. Three times the New Testament writers quote this verse (Romans 1:17, Galatians 3:11, and Hebrews 10:38-39). For *"without faith it is impossible to please Him, for he who comes to God must believe that He is, and that He is a rewarder of those who diligently seek Him"* (Hebrews 11:6). I don't know about you, but I want to please God with my faith. I want to believe God, trust Him, and grow in my faith. The Bible tells us that *"faith comes by hearing and hearing by the Word of God"* (Romans 10:17). Our faith grows when we hear, read, and believe the Word, walking *"by faith, not by sight"* (2 Corinthians 5:7).

Have you ever felt like God promised you something but it's been so long in coming? Maybe too long? Perhaps you're feeling desperate and even despairing. Maybe you've asked questions like Habakkuk – why, Lord? What are you doing? Why are you silent? How can you do this and be consistent with who You are? We've all had quandaries of the soul. And it is in such times that we, by faith, are called to seek Him in worship. In praise. With a heart of gratitude as we look to the past, and like Habakkuk, magnifying His attributes and names (*"Everlasting, Holy One, O Rock"*) as we trust Him for our past, present, and future. For we, the just, live by our faith.

Your Story Matters: Just in Christ

"For I am not ashamed of the gospel of Christ, for it is the power of God to salvation for everyone who believes, for the Jew first and also for the Greek. For in it the righteousness of God is revealed from faith to faith as it is written, 'the just shall live by faith'" (Romans 1:16-17).

Early in my Christian faith, I heard a metaphor regarding salvation that still resonates with me today. Think of the goodness of human beings, like buildings we observe from the ground. Some individuals, like the tallest building in the world (currently Burj Khalfia in Dubai at 2,717 feet), seem to reach the sky in their goodness, virtue, and morality. While others, the evil among us, never rise above sea level. Somewhere in-between, the vast majority fall, worse than "the best" (Peter? Paul?), but definitely better than the "the worst" (Judas? Hitler?). And yet, from another perspective, say a heavenly one, every building, regardless of height, appears exceptionally flat. Whether you're flying at 35,000 feet or reaching the altitude of SpaceX at 130 miles, every human's feeble DIY attempt to reach God falls woefully short. A chasm no human construction effort will ever span. Indeed, we need a supernatural bridge built by God to reach God.

The finished work of Jesus Christ was precisely the divine intervention our sinful souls needed. Christ, our only hope for salvation, and the gospel the means by which the power of God is displayed. The word *gospel* most simply means "good news." And, of course, no news can be defined as good unless there first be corresponding bad news. And here it is: Each of us is a building, and regardless of our height, our sin causes us to fall infinitely short of God. And there's nothing we can do. Sure, we can spend the rest of our lives adding a story or two, but at the end of the day, we're still left with the chasm. Or, we can believe in the One who died for us, the perfect one who absorbed our sins and bore the wrath of God so we might live.

You decide: Faith in Him or faith in yourself? Do you keep futilely constructing your building, or do you put your faith in the One who already built the perfect bridge? And even then, your faith in Him is a gift from Him, *"For by grace you have been saved through faith, and that not of yourselves, it is the gift of God"* (Ephesians 2:8). Because "every *good and perfect gift comes from above"* (James 1:17), so also has the gift of faith been given to you.

"We love because He first loved us" (1 John 4:19). To God be the glory, great things He has done!

Your Story Matters:
Christ + Nothing = Life

"But that no one is justified by the law in the sight of God is evident, for 'the just shall live by faith'" (Galatians 3:11).

Here, we find the second time Habakkuk 2:4 is referenced in the New Testament. Faith is not only a prerequisite for salvation but also our foundation for living. The Hebrew word for *live* is *chaya,* which means *"to stay alive; to be preserved to flourish; to enjoy life; to live in happiness; to breathe; to be alive; to be animated; to recover health; to live continuously."* The just shall live continuously by faith. Not drawing upon it from time to time, but 24/7/365.

During his early missionary travels, Paul went to Galatia (modern-day Turkey) and planted many churches in the region. He preached the gospel (Romans 1:16-17), and the churches grew and were soundly established. However, after some time, news came back to Paul that those who had begun in faith were ceasing to live by it. Incorporating Jewish ordinances, they essentially said, *"Faith may have been all right as a beginning when we were new Christians, but now we must add works to our faith."* Paul was flabbergasted! He wrote back immediately to warn that they had adopted a different gospel. A false gospel. A gospel that was not good news at all but one of enslavement. He asks them, *"Who has bewitched you... did you receive the Spirit by the works of the law or by the hearing of faith?* (Galatians 3:1-2).

Paul instructed that rather than justifying a person before God, the Law curses them because it makes demands no one can keep. Through His death on the cross, Christ did for us what we could not do ourselves. His work—not ours—removed the curse upon us, given our inability to obey the Law. The only way to live is the same way we were saved: By faith in Christ alone. From that faith, good works emanate (Ephesians 2:10), not as a condition for salvation but as a by-product of (James 2:14-26). Why? Because healthy trees produce good fruit. They can't help themselves. That's why Paul described these outcomes of faith as *"the fruit of the Spirit"* (Galatians 5:22).

Christ alone for salvation and living the Christian life: *"I have been crucified with Christ; it is no longer I who live, but Christ lives in me; and the life which I now live in the flesh I live by faith in the Son of God, who loved me and gave Himself for me"* (Galatians 2:20). *"Christ in you, the hope of glory"* (Colossians 1:27).

Your Story Matters: The Life Well Lived

"'Now the just shall live by faith; but if anyone draws back, My soul has no pleasure in him.' But we are not of those who draw back to perdition, but of those who believe to the saving of the soul" (Hebrews 10:38-39).

The final time we see Habakkuk 2:4 quoted in the New Testament is as a preamble to the great "Hall of Faith" chapter of Hebrews 11, where everyone mentioned is united by a common thread: faith. What isn't a common thread is the many different circumstances in which faith manifested. We all love where *"faith subdued kingdoms, worked righteousness, obtained promises, stopped the mouths of lions, became valiant in battle"* (Hebrews 11:33-34). Yay! But what about the others who manifested their faith in being *"tortured, chains, imprisonments, stoned, sawn in two, slain with the sword, destitute, afflicted, tormented"* (Hebrews 11:35-37)? Not so much yay. And yet, here they all are, commended in the Hall of Faith. Why? Because they pleased God. *"But without faith it is impossible to please Him, for he who comes to God must believe that He is, and that He is a rewarder of those who diligently seek Him"* (Hebrews 11:6).

And so, God rewards faith. Those who diligently seek Him. The question is, how does this *reward* appear, and what does it look like? If you are like me, my mind naturally defaults to good things, like ice cream when we're young, and perhaps monetary or recognition rewards when we're older. Perks. Bennies. But tortured? Sawn in two? Destitute? Tormented? Sounds like more of a penalty to me. So how were all these members of the Hall of Faith rewarded?

When God appeared to Abram in a vision, He told him, *"Do not be afraid, Abram, I am your shield, your exceedingly great reward"* (Genesis 15:1). Elsewhere we read, *"You will show me the path of life; in your presence is fullness of joy"* (Psalm 16:11), *"Whom have I in heaven but You? And there is none upon earth that I desire besides You"* (Psalm 73:25). Jesus assured us *"Lo I am with you always, even to the end of the age"* (Matthew 28:20). *He* is our exceedingly great reward. Whether you are experiencing the joy of an obtained promise or are in the depths of a painful affliction, Jesus is with you. Faith is believing He is. Here, in every moment throughout our earthly pilgrimage, and there, when our faith will turn to sight, and we will see Him, face to face.

Your Story Matters: Neener, Neener, Neener

"Will not all these take up a proverb against him, and a taunting riddle against him, and say, woe to him who increases what is not his – how long? And to him who loads himself with many pledges" (Habakkuk 2:6).

Habakkuk 2:6-20 is what is called a taunt song. A literary genre that expresses public humiliation and scorn for the misfortune of a person or group. Taunt songs are filled with the kind of mockery and derision one might hear from children celebrating the defeat of the playground bully (thus the sophisticated title of this devotional). Probably the most famous taunt song in our day and age is the equally mature, *Na Na Hey Hey Kiss Him Goodbye*, a song released in 1969 by Steam and sung many times by many a home crowd against the losing visiting team. In essence, declaring, *"You came here thinking you'd win, but in the end, you lost, so goodbye, you loser."* In the taunt song of Habakkuk 2, we have five stanzas of *woe* revealing the misery awaiting the Chaldeans:

1. **Greed (v. 6-8)** – The natural but destructive fruit of a nation that does not trust God. These verses communicate the outcome of those who live by stolen goods and extortion.
2. **Coveting (v. 9-11)** – Wanting what belongs to someone else. There will be no ultimate peace for the nation that acquires by evil gain.
3. **Violence (v. 12-14)** – Greed digresses to coveting, which digresses to violence. Like Ahab greedily coveting Naboth's vineyard but failing to acquire it, he had his wife Jezebel murder him (1 Kings 21).
4. **Seduction (v. 15-17)** – Having attained by violence what they coveted, drunk in their victory, shame and violence will be their downfall.
5. **Idolatry (v. 18-20)** – The false, idolatrous gods of the Chaldeans will not save them in the day of God's retribution and wrath.

Like nations, turning away from the one true God will ultimately leave us in ruin and defeat. Made in God's image, we are wired for fellowship and relationship with Him alone. This is the contrast laid out for us in Habakkuk chapter 2: Live by faith in the One who alone justifies, or live by sight and your own manipulative devising. You choose. May we, and all nations, be wise in heeding the profound benediction closing this chapter, *"The Lord is in His holy temple, let all the earth keep silence before Him* (Habakkuk 2:20). For in the end, He wins, and *"The earth will be filled with the knowledge of the glory of the Lord, as the waters cover the sea"* (Habakkuk 2:14).

Christ in the Old

"The genuine believer takes the whole of Scripture as a living organism produced by the Holy Spirit to present Christ to him. On every page of Scripture, he finds traits and traces of the Mediator."

Geerhardus Vos

True Value

"See, I have called by name Bezalel the son of Uri, the son of Hur, of the tribe of Judah. And I have filled him with the Spirit of God, in wisdom, in understanding, in knowledge, and in all manner of workmanship, to design artistic works" (Exodus 31:2-4).

Our world has a very misguided way of assigning worth to people. It seems we humans have this almost subconscious grading system, a "caste system" of sorts when it comes to placing value on others. Unfortunately, believers are not immune from this innate tendency. If we're completely honest, don't we think some are more valuable than others in the church? "Surely," we assume, "those gifted to teach and speak publicly are the ones who are truly being used by God, vs. us 'less important' folks who anonymously serve in the shadows." "The ones on stage and in the limelight are the ones making the greatest impact and having the broadest influence," we surmise. By placing those in key leadership roles on a pedestal, how susceptible we are to minimize our own less prominent contributions.

When reading the book of Exodus, we can probably name the show's main star: Moses. But who remembers Bezalel and his assistant Aholiab? Filled with the Spirit of God, their contributions were not to teach or be famous keynote speakers. No, they were filled with the Spirit for embroidery, engraving, carving wood, and mounting gemstones. Making tangible products with divine excellence.

In Christ, you too are filled with the Spirit of God, in all wisdom, knowledge, and understanding. And God has called you to serve in the body of Christ, having equal value and importance as those assigned to more leading roles, for a body needs EVERY part. So don't mentally or verbally diminish your contribution or your value. Instead, take God at His word: *"Those members of the body which seem to be weaker are necessary. And those members of the body which we think to be less honorable, on these we bestow greater honor"* (I Corinthians 12:22-23).

Lost at Sea

"Once again you will have compassion on us. You will trample our sins under your feet and throw them into the depths of the ocean!" (Micah 7:19).

The Mariana Trench is located in the western Pacific Ocean, about 124 miles from the Mariana Islands. This crescent-shaped trench is about 1,580 miles in length, and at the southern end, there is a small valley with a floor known as Challenger Deep, the deepest seabed on Earth. Descending 35,856 feet down, Challenger Deep is 1.2 miles farther from sea level than the peak of Mt. Everest. While Micah may not have known the specifics of the Mariana Trench, when it comes to God throwing your sins into the ocean's depths, the Challenger Deep provides a clear picture of where your sins are in Christ.

There are two lessons we can learn from this passage in Micah. First, note that your sins are not near the shoreline. They've been cast into the *depths* of the ocean. Where you stand on the beach, your sins cannot be seen. Even with binoculars. Second, your sins are not floating on the surface. Despite chartering a ship and scouring every nautical mile of the ocean, you will never find any of your sins buoyantly floating on the surface. They are gone, having disappeared from sight into the *depths* of the sea. This is the power of the cross and the finished work of Jesus Christ. Oh, and BTW: God has posted a "No Fishing" sign for this, His ocean of love.

From the hymn *O The Deep, Deep Love of Jesus:*

> O the deep, deep love of Jesus – Love of every love the best!
> Tis an ocean vast of blessing, Tis a haven sweet of rest.
> O the deep, deep love of Jesus – Tis a heav'n of heav'ns to me;
> And it lifts me up to glory, For it lifts me, Lord to Thee!

Finishing Strong

"But King Solomon loved many foreign women….and he had seven hundred wives, princesses, and three hundred concubines; and his wives turned away his heart. For it was so, when Solomon was old, that his wives turned his heart after other gods; and his heart was not loyal to the Lord his God"
(1 Kings 11:1, 3-4).

When Marjie and I were newly married, our pastor preached a sermon on the life of King Solomon that left an indelible mark on my life. Solomon, he taught, started so strongly in life, gifted with unsurpassed divine wisdom, enabling him to write Psalm 72, the bulk of Proverbs, Song of Solomon, and the book of Ecclesiastes. And yet, in the end, he had allowed his *"foreign wives"* to influence his heart towards God. Tripping and falling just before the finish line, Solomon is an example of how *not* to complete the race of life we've each been given here on Earth.

While I will never have seven hundred wives or three hundred concubines, I have had many "loves" that have attempted to pull me away from my first love, Jesus Christ. If you are like me, you too have many *"foreign women"* in your life seeking to tempt and entice you away from your first love: Greed, envy, selfish ambition, pride, money, and the praise of man, to name just a few. Or as Jesus taught, *"…the cares of this world, the deceitfulness of riches, and the desires for other things…"* (Mark 4:19).

So let's heed the exhortation of Paul in 1 Corinthians 9:24-27, finishing our race strong, running *"in such a way as to get the prize,"* having hearts remaining loyal to the Lord our God to the very end.

As You Wish

"This is the day the Lord has made; we will rejoice and be glad in it"
(Psalm 118:24).

If you are a goal-oriented, target-driven person, that's a good thing. Because, as you know, if you aim at nothing, you'll surely hit it. But, like most things in life, having this strength may also be one of your greatest weaknesses. The downside of goal orientation is its propensity to take us out of the moment, causing us to see the present as merely a means to an end. Wishing away the moment because of the destination we have in mind. Take child-rearing, for example. When you feel like a sherpa during the infant years – as you put them in the car seat for the millionth time – you may long for the day when they can get in by themselves. Being single, and all you can think about is the happiness marriage will bring. Struggling with contentment at work because the long-awaited promotion has been so elusive. Or seeing the tropical vacation on your calendar, and the days can't seem to go fast enough. Goals, targets, ends, and destinations are not without their impact.

In his 1841 essay "Self-Reliance," Ralph Waldo Emerson spoke to this danger of thinking the future destination holds the key to our happiness:

"At home I dream that at Naples, at Rome, I can be intoxicated with beauty, and lose my sadness. I pack my trunk, embrace my friends, embark on the sea, and at last wake up in Naples, and there beside me is the stern fact, the sad self, unrelenting, identical, that I fled from."

While wishing for things and having an end in mind may have its place, be aware of its downside impact. For maybe God intends the means to *be* the end. And perhaps the journey *is* the destination. For learning to be in the moment and finding our joy and happiness there is distinctly possible for those in Christ. Why? Because He is there. In the moment. Every moment. Jesus promised, *"Lo, I am with you always, even to the end of the age"* (Matthew 28:20), and David assures us, *"In Your presence is fullness of joy"* (Psalm 16:11). The past we can hand off to God, and the future we entrust to Him. So let's live in the moment, for *"You maintain my lot, the lines have fallen to me in pleasant places; yes, I have a good inheritance"* (Psalm 16:5-6).

Today, in this very moment, as you read, the lines have fallen to you in pleasant places.

Living Among Us

"Then I will live among the people of Israel and be their God, and they will know that I am the Lord their God. I am the one who brought them out of the land of Egypt so that I could live among them. I am the Lord their God"
(Exodus 29:45-46 NLT).

Birthed during the Age of Enlightenment, Deism is a philosophical system of thought that believes a supreme being created the universe and then stepped away, allowing it to be run by its own natural laws. Denying the supernatural and the divinity of Jesus Christ, deists believe the creator is like a great watchmaker who, after creating the world and winding it up like a watch, now aloofly stands aside to let it mechanistically run on its own. Believing in a creator who does not intervene in the universe or interact with humanity, this rationalistic position from the 17th and 18th centuries starkly contrasts the God revealed in the Bible.

The story of Scripture is the story of God's intentional revelation over His creation and to His people. Ultimately culminating in Him becoming one of us. *"'Behold, the virgin shall be with child, and bear a Son, and they shall call His name Immanuel,' which is translated, 'God with us'"* (Matthew 1:23). Rather than being uninvolved or disinterested, our Heavenly Father is the polar opposite of deistic thought. In Christ, our Abba Father is permanently and constantly available for intimacy, relationship, and communion with His sons and daughters.

"The Lord is near to those who have a broken heart" (Psalm 34:18).

"Blessed be the God and Father of our Lord Jesus Christ, the Father of mercies and the God of all comfort, who comforts us in all our tribulation…..for as the sufferings of Christ abound in us, so our consolation also abounds through Christ" (1 Corinthians 1:3-5).

So let's draw near to Him, for He has drawn near to us.

Strangers in our Midst

"You shall neither mistreat a stranger nor oppress him, for you were strangers in the land of Egypt" (Exodus 22:21).

Birds of a feather flock together. Haven't we all experienced that in life? Either from being on the inside looking out or from the outside looking in. In high school, we called them "cliques". Like being with like. Uniformity in our affiliations. Remember the jocks, stoners, cheerleaders, loners, and nerds? Group memberships formed from shared interests, body types, and/or personalities. You would think that once we grew out of our youthful insecurities and matured, diversity would be more common in our relational connections. Especially as believers. But sadly, especially in the ever-increasingly polarized society in which we live, the practice of high school remains. Only the associations have changed.

In the above passage, God roots his protection of the stranger in empathy, reminding the Israelites to remember their own experience as powerless slaves in Egypt. Empathy is what attracts us to the widow and orphan. The new student at school, the visitor at church, the immigrant, the new co-worker, or the new neighbor. As we walk in their shoes, remembering what it's like to be invisible, lonely, or marginalized, empathy will enable us to build those bridges rather than the natural walls of exclusion we so quickly erect. Jesus Himself said, *"By this all will know that you are my disciples, if you have love for one another"* (John 13:35).

True, associating only with those who think and act as we do is more convenient. It enables us to stay frozen where we are, taking the easier path versus the rough terrain of change and adaptation. And yet, God has called us into His body, organically connected to all the many diverse members of that one body,

"But now indeed there are many members, yet one body. And the eye cannot say to the hand, 'I have no need of you'; nor again the head to the feet, 'I have no need of you'" (I Corinthians 12:20-21).

So let's be bridge builders, for we *"are all one in Christ Jesus"* (Galatians 3:28).

Be Brave:
Before Rahab Went to Rehab

"I know that the Lord has given you this land and that a great fear of you has fallen on us, so that all who live in this country are melting in fear because of you. Now then, please swear to me by the Lord that you will show kindness to my family, because I have shown kindness to you" (Joshua 2:9, 12).

Impossible circumstances. Impossible odds. Rahab was in an impossible predicament with no hope and no future. Working as a prostitute in Jericho, news had spread quickly that the God of the Israelites was about to destroy her city. In just a few short days, Rahab was about to become yet another unnamed casualty. A wartime statistic. Jericho was a city without Sabbaths.... God's Word was never read...and no prophets with a message of a coming Messiah ever spoke. Rahab was one woman alone with the grime of too many nights on her hands and the weight of too many wounds on her heart. Impossible, wouldn't you say?

Until God showed up in the form of the two spies. God, who can reveal Himself wherever, whenever, and to whomever. God who is never limited by our spirit of lack or restricted only for the expectant. God, who is no respecter of persons, gives the gift of faith in the most impossible situations. He alone sovereignly led the spies to the one person in Jericho who believed in Him. Hebrews 11:31 later tells us, *"By faith the prostitute Rahab, because she welcomed the spies, was not killed with those who were disobedient."*

It is so important to see that Rahab's exercise of faith did not come *after* she went to rehab! She never read anything, did not attend church, and had no special angelic visitations. Rehab believed in the God of the Hebrews amid her impossible situation while making a living as a prostitute. How can this be? *"God demonstrates His own love for us in that while we were still sinners, Christ died for us"* (Romans 5:8). That is how. For with God, all things are possible.

Be Brave:
Before Rahab Went to Rehab (continued)

"Now the men had said to her, 'This oath you made us swear will not be binding on us unless, when we enter the land, you have tied this scarlet cord in the window.' 'Agreed,' she replied, 'Let it be as you say.' So she sent them away, and they departed. And she tied the scarlet cord in the window" (Joshua 2:17-18, 21).

Rahab lives in a godless place with a godless past, with a seemingly impossible situation with little promise or hope. But she fully believes, and because of this, she begins to fully live. She steps out in faith and serves her enemies, providing the most incredible gift someone can give to future generations: A lineage of grace. Rahab, the scarlet woman, throws a scarlet cord out her window – the one thread that everything is hanging on – and is delivered by that single scarlet cord, tying her into the Jewish people and the family of God forever. For in the lineage of Jesus Christ, we read, *"Salmon begot Boaz by Rahab, Boaz begot Obed by Ruth, Obed begot Jesse, and Jesse begot David the king"* (Matthew 1:5)

And who came from King David's royal line? Our very own Messiah, Jesus the Christ. God makes the former woman of the night into a woman of the court! A princess and the wife of a Jewish prince, Salmon. Rahab is one of only a handful of women named in the genealogy leading straight to Jesus Christ. The One who is the actual scarlet cord on which everything hangs. Running throughout the Bible, you'll find His redemptive work wherever you look. And, if you belong to Him, there is a scarlet cord of redemption running through your life too. Not only redeeming your past but also providing hope for your future. Like Rehab, let's take God at His Word and see the fog of impossibility blasted away from our lives.

From the hymn *Redeemed:*

> *Redeemed how I love to proclaim it,*
> *redeemed by the blood of the Lamb!*
> *Redeemed thru His infinite mercy,*
> *His child and forever I am.*

Standing Alone

"Our God whom we serve is able to deliver us from the burning fiery furnace, and He will deliver us from your hand, O king. But if not, let it be known to you, O king, that we do not serve your gods, or will we worship the gold image which you have set up" (Daniel 3:17-18).

I heard a story once about a teacher who took a fish out of its bowl and left a classroom of children as it flopped around. He told them they would be expelled if anyone left their seat. All of the children sat and watched as the fish flopped around, gasping for air. No one wanted to get up to avoid getting in trouble. Finally, a boy sprang up from his seat and ran to the fish, placing it back in the bowl. Ultimately, he was the only one who refused to watch the fish die. When the teacher returned, he told the class this was the lesson: The fear of getting in trouble should never stop you from doing what is right. Sometimes, you may have to oppose authority and groupthink simply because it's the right thing to do.

Standing alone in doing the right thing comes in all shapes and sizes. Sometimes, it may be small; other times, it may be big. Sometimes, it may be in private; other times, it may be very public. Sometimes, the consequences are inconsequential; other times, they may involve your life. Like it did with Shadrach, Meshack, and Abed-Nego in the book of Daniel. However, the one consistency is that doing the right thing is timeless. Like those three who stood up in the Old Testament, Peter tells the high priest in the New Testament, *"We ought to obey God rather than men"* (Acts 5:29) when commanded not to talk about Jesus.

So when the time comes for you, be ready to put the fish back in the bowl.

Transitioning to your Next Destination

"Moses My servant is dead. Now therefore, arise, go over this Jordan, you and all this people, to the land which I am giving them – the children of Israel" (Joshua 1:2).

I vividly remember when we were about to sit down for dinner as a new couple with our little girl. Having been tasked to inform her of this joyous news, I was completely blindsided when she burst into great weeping, wailing, and gnashing of teeth upon receiving this terrible blow. It seems she was highly engrossed in a game, and I had the audacity to bring it to a quick and cataclysmic end. Lesson learned. In the future, we will forever implement the parental *"OK, in five minutes, we're going to _____."* Unfortunately, life is not always that kind. Like my dinner announcement, life can throw us abrupt and unexpected curveballs. Like the one Joshua received: Moses is dead. You're the leader. Go.

Transition periods can be difficult. We know we're not where we were, which may have been comfortable and safe, and yet we're not at our destination either. How will we respond to the transition times in our lives? Here are three principles we can glean from Joshua chapter one to help us with our own seasons of change.

First and foremost, God is the One who does the work. He goes before us, behind us, and will get us to where He has always planned us to be. Trust in Him and lean not on your own understanding. *"Be strong and of good courage; do not be afraid, not be dismayed, for the Lord your God is with you wherever you go"* (Joshua 1:9).

Second, fight destiny malaise. Having wandered for forty years in the desert, the people could easily have stayed stuck, focusing on the negative and their lack: regretting the past, wishing things were different, refusing to change, or possessing the mindset, *"things will never change."* Look through the windshield of life and not your rearview mirror.

And finally, sometimes, it's the small steps of obedience God asks us to take that will propel us through these transitional seasons and into our destiny. Here, the people are told to *"prepare provisions for yourselves"* and to *"remember the Word the Lord commanded you."* And their response? *"All that you command us we will do."* May we respond in a like manner, for obedience is the great opener of eyes enabling us to see the path ahead.

Fill in the Blank

"For thus says the High and Lofty One who inhabits eternity, whose name is Holy; I dwell in the high and holy place……….." (Isaiah 57:15).

Now, no cheating: Without reading ahead, fill in the above verse from Isaiah. In this passage, the Lord is about to communicate His point of connection with those made in His image. In my mind, brace for impact! When I take in words such as *High* and *Lofty One* and *eternity* and *Holy*, I conjure up images from Jonathan Edwards's 1741 sermon, *Sinners in the Hands of an Angry God.* Infinitely perfect in who He is and in all His ways, I see a scary, vivid, and infinite contrast between He who is high and lifted up, and we finite, sinful human beings who are but dust. Wouldn't it be natural to project onto the Lord what we do with our vast human contrasts and divides? The rich looking down on the poor. The beautiful disdaining the ugly. The powerful scorning the weak.

OK, now you can look. Here's the answer to our little test, *"…….with him who has a contrite and humble spirit, to revive the spirit of the humble, and to revive the heart of the contrite ones."* How counterintuitive to our human way of thinking! Our Mighty and Holy and Eternal God dwells not only in heaven but with the contrite, those who have been crushed and broken in life and by life.

Is that you? If it is, and you are in Christ, He has chosen you as His friend, to live and make His home, not only in heaven, but in you. For this is who He is. This is the very heart of God:

*"Come to me, all you who labor and are heavy laden, and I will give you rest. Take my yoke upon you and learn from Me, for **I am gentle and lowly in heart**, and you will find rest for your souls. For my yoke is easy and My burden is light"* (Matthew 11:28-30).

Desperate Measures

"In her deep anguish Hannah prayed to the Lord, weeping bitterly"
(1 Samuel 1:10).

In the book of Samuel, we are told about Elkanah and his two wives, Peninnah and Hannah. Peninnah had children, but Hannah was barren. Day after day, year after year, Peninnah would mock, tease, and taunt Hannah about her barrenness. Finally, one year something snapped in Hannah, and she could take it no longer. In deep anguish of soul, she cried out to God in prayer. In her prayer, she promised God that if He gave her a son, she would dedicate him to the Lord for as long as he lived. Amid the dark culture and society of Hannah's day, we see a desperate, simple woman stirred to pray a prayer that will ultimately usher in a new day in Israel's future and change world history, for she would give birth to the prophet Samuel.

Hannah's prayer was, in essence, "Lord, make me fruitful, or I don't want to go on." God wanted her story told in detail so future generations would recognize Israel's turnaround started with a lonely, heartbroken woman who just wanted to bear fruit. This story is about so much more than a woman who is praying for a child. Although it is that, this is about the power of fervent prayer asked in a spirit of faith. Hannah reminds us not to hesitate to cry out to God when we want to bear fruit for Him and see Jesus shine in our worlds – in our homes, schools, families, friendships, and businesses. Hannah travailed in prayer and bore fruit. In the New Testament, Paul said something similar: *"I travail like a mother giving birth until Christ be formed in you"* (Galatians 4:19).

Isn't that what we all want? To see Jesus formed in us, and see Him brilliantly displayed throughout our dark world.

Leah's Story: When Morning Comes

"When morning came, there was Leah!" (Genesis 29:25).

You'll want to read the entirety of Genesis 29 to understand the story we'll be going over these next few days. While at first glance you may think this is a love story between Jacob and Rachel, it's, in fact, a chronicle about the purpose of God emerging out of a *very* messy family situation. Something I'm sure we can all relate to.

As the story goes, Jacob arrives at his grandfather's hometown, and the first place he comes to is a well. Along comes Rachel to water her sheep, and Jacob is immediately transfixed with her beauty. They begin talking and discover they are related. Rachel runs to tell her dad Laban, and soon it's one big, happy family reunion. Laban also has an older daughter named Leah. One who has *"weak eyes".* Not sure what that means, but we do know it was Rachel who was *"lovely in form and was beautiful."* Rachel was the one with the stunning beauty, while the unattractive and invisible Leah was the one Jacob and all the other men looked right past. And if Leah had any doubt as to her inferiority, she only had to think of their names. Rachel means *"ewe,"* and Leah means *"cow."*

The years pass, and the wedding day for Jacob and Rachel arrives. The scheming Laban plots to sneak the weak-eyed Leah into the bridal chamber for the honeymoon night, hoping Jacob does not discover it until the morning. And somehow, he doesn't. *"When morning came, there was Leah!"* Six angering words for Jacob and six heart-breaking words for Leah.

Can you relate? When morning came, there was _____. When morning came, there was fear. There was dread and apprehension. When morning came, there was the heartache over my failed marriage, the rejection I feel, the job I hate to go to, my current health crises, the pain of my wayward child, or the tension of my ongoing addiction. What do you face every morning, and how do you face it? *"Why are you cast down, O my soul? And why are you disquieted within me? Hope in God, for I shall yet praise Him"* (Psalm 42:5).

Leah's Story:
The Lord Sees

"Now when the Lord saw that Leah was unloved, He made her able to bear children, but Rachel was barren" (Genesis 29:31).

Wedded to Leah, Jacob worked another seven years for Uncle Laban to have Rachel's hand in marriage. With Jacob and Rachel finally together, Leah now felt truly rejected and unloved. But the Lord saw her, and kindness showed up for Leah in the most amazing way. Desperate to be loved, she soon realized she alone could bear children. Surely, this would prove to her husband she was worth something. She was worth being loved and pursued. She did have a purpose! Deep inside her soul, Leah desired someone to see beyond her *"weak eyes"* and love her for who she was – a daughter of God, created in His image.

Reading further, *"Leah became pregnant and gave birth to a son. She named him Reuben, for she said, 'It is because the Lord has seen my misery. Surely my husband will love me now'"* (Genesis 29:32). Leah's journey into motherhood reveals a great deal about her spiritual journey, for in Hebrew culture a name has significance, revealing the character of the bearer and/or giver of the name. The name *Reuben* sounds like the Hebrew words *"the Lord has seen my misery"* and literally means *"see a son."* Her firstborn son's birth reminded Leah that God was not blind to her needs. He had seen her profound misery and sent her a blessing, someone she could see and love.

"She conceived again, and when she gave birth to a son she said, 'Because the Lord heard that I am not loved, He gave me this one too.' So she named him Simeon. Again she conceived, and when she gave birth to a son she said, 'Now at last my husband will become attached to me, because I have borne him three sons.' So he was named Levi" (Genesis 29:33-34). Still craving her husband's attention and attachment, Leah was experiencing God's concern for her in practical terms. The Lord provided companionship and love through her sons when her husband did not.

And yet, somewhere between verse 34 and verse 35, something radically changed in Leah. She was about to identify the true source of her value, meaning, and purpose. What she had been searching for all her life. Leah's days of defining herself by the names and labels others gave her were about to end.

Leah's Story:
This Time I Will Praise the Lord

"Again she conceived and gave birth to a fourth son, and she said, 'This time I will praise the Lord'" (Genesis 29:35a).

This time, I will praise the Lord! What a huge turning point in her life. This time…. I will find my identity in the One who loves me, knows me, and has a purpose for my life. This time…. I will look up at my Redeemer with praise and not look down on myself in shame. This time…. I will be defined as a woman loved deeply by my Lord.

Where *we* are able to say: Though my husband doesn't love me, yet I will praise the Lord. Though my friend has rejected me, yet I will praise the Lord. Though I don't know how I'm going to pay for this, yet I will praise the Lord. This is called a sacrifice of praise. Praising God when we don't feel like it…. even amid the very hard things of life.

Every sacrifice of praise has a *though* and a *yet*. *"Though He slay me, yet will I praise Him"* (Job 13:15). *"Though the fig tree does not blossom; and there is no fruit on the vines…. yet I will choose to rejoice in the Lord; I will choose to shout in exultation in the victorious God of my salvation"* (Habakkuk 3:17-18). Have you had a *though* and a *yet* moment in your life? Do you have one now? Throughout the Bible, the stories of praising the Lord during trouble and heartache reveal the breakthrough presence of God and His loving care, kindness, and compassion. We see it when the children of Israel shouted with a voice of praise, and the walls of Jericho came tumbling down. We see it when Jehoshaphat sent the choir out in front of the army to praise the Lord, and their enemies were defeated. And we see it in the story of Paul and Silas in prison. Bruised and beaten, the Bible tells us at midnight, sitting there in the darkness, they were singing hymns of praise to God. *Before* their chains fell off.

In the end, Leah came to realize only God could fill the God-shaped void she had in her soul. *"The Lord is my strength and my shield. Therefore my heart greatly rejoices, and with my heart I will praise Him"* (Psalm 28:7).

Leah's Story:
The Lion of the Tribe of Judah

"So she named him Judah" (Genesis 29:35b).

And that fourth son? The one whose very name means *praise*? Judah became the tribe that would bring about the royal line. King David would descend from Judah, as would Solomon, and so would a man named Joseph, the earthly father of the Christ child Jesus. Jesus came from Leah's seed! Leah – the one with the weak eyes. The one who was invisible, unwanted, rejected, hurt, and disappointed – that Leah would become the very ancestor of the Lord Jesus Christ. Out of Judah comes Jesus, who, in every action, detail, and word of His life, is a praise to His Father.

You see? This is what our great God does! He takes the messiness of our lives and makes them our messages of love, joy, and redemption in Him. He takes the seemingly ordinary people who might not look like they can accomplish much, and He makes them extraordinary, becoming a part of God's redemptive plan for our broken world. For, in the end, Leah could conclude, "This time I will praise the Lord and allow Him to define me!"

As we close the story of Leah, remember we are all children of light. Refuse to believe God won't use you for His purposes. Regardless of your background, story, pain, family of origin, or even the current hard things you might be dealing with, you can declare: "Though my life is difficult right now, I *will* praise the Lord." This is the sacrifice of praise! Your life matters to God, and today is the day to align with His plans and purposes, trusting Him for your past, present, and future, so you too can flourish and shine like Leah.

The Slippery Slope

"Catch us the foxes, the little foxes that spoil the vine"
(Song of Solomon 2:15).

No one ever wakes up in the morning and says, "Gee, I think I'll go to work today and embezzle $300,000." More likely, it's a progression, beginning with "small" things such as using the copier for personal reasons. A favorite example of mine comes from George Lefcoe, the former Los Angeles County Regional Planning Commissioner, who offered the following thoughts on his retirement and the seduction of public office:

> "I really missed the cards from engineers I never met, the wine and cheese from development companies I never heard of, and the honey-baked ham from, all places, a cemetery. My first Christmas as commissioner – when I received the ham – I tried to return it, though for the record, I did not, since no one at the cemetery seemed authorized to accept the ham. When I received another ham the next Christmas, I gave it to a worthy charity. The next year, some worthy friends were having a party so I gave it to them. The next year I had a party and we enjoyed the ham. In the fifth year, about the tenth of December, I began to wonder, where is my ham?"

How does one go from an absolute standard of accepting nothing—indeed, returning the gift—to expecting the gift? Maybe a metaphor closer to home would be the purchase of a new car. What began as "No food or drink in the car!" evolved to "Well, ok, you can have a drink, but don't spill it" and ended up ten years later discovering prehistoric french fries under the seat.

Ethical and moral lines are never static but dynamic. And if we could trace back significant moral failures to their origin, we undoubtedly would find one of those pesky little foxes. So what guard has God given us so we don't begin this slippery descent? The person and light of Jesus Christ. *"But if we walk in the light as He is in the light, we have fellowship with one another; and the blood of Jesus Christ His Son cleanses us from all sin. If we confess our sins, He is faithful and just to forgive us our sins and to cleanse us from all unrighteousness"* (1 John 1:7, 9).

While integrity can be defined as what you do when no one is watching, it is also true that Someone always is. The Light of the World is also our Bright Morning Star, so let's always walk with Him in His loving, merciful, life-giving, warm, and comforting light.

Becoming a Son of Merari

"Their only duty at the Tabernacle will be to carry loads"
(Numbers 4:31 NLT).

Have you ever wondered how all the articles of the Tabernacle moved during the forty years of wandering by the children of Israel in the desert? And did you know the total weight of the Tabernacle was over eight tons, according to some estimates? Well, if you are like me, you probably haven't given this much consideration. That is until I read the account of the sons of Merari (Numbers 4:29-33), who were tasked to carry the bulk of this heavy load through the hot desert all those many years. Now, as someone who has moved and helped others to move, I know the way to go is to take the shortest route when carrying a heavy load. Not for the poor sons of Merari. They kept going in circles……. for forty years! Weight, heat, and route: Everything was stacked against them. But faithfully carrying the load they did, and eventually, all the articles safely reached their Promised Land.

As believers in Christ, we too have been tasked to carry the load: The load and burden of others. *"Bear one another's burdens, and so fulfill the law of Christ"* (Galatians 6:2). In the body of Christ, no man or woman is an island unto themselves. While Americans may think of themselves as "rugged individualists," the Bible says Christians are members of each other. Meaning that we are dependently connected to the point where we *"Rejoice with those who rejoice, and weep with those who weep"* (Romans 12:15).

As we grow in Jesus, spiritual maturity transitions us from being served to contributing members of Christ's body serving others. Unlike the recipients of the letter to the Hebrews: *"For by this time you ought to be teachers, you need someone to teach you again the first principles of the oracles of God; and you have come to need milk and not solid food"* (Hebrews 5:12).

If you are an adult in Christ, it's time to be mature and eat solid food. It's time to serve others and bear their burdens. And this can only be accomplished (and sustained) by first wearing the life-giving yoke of Christ. *"Take my yoke upon you and learn from Me, for I am gentle and lowly of heart, and you will find rest for your souls. For my yoke is easy and My burden is light"* (Matthew 11:29-30).

In taking on His yoke daily, we will be supernaturally empowered *"for the equipping of the saints for the work of ministry"* (Ephesians 4:12), carrying their burdens so we as an entire body can all safely reach the true Promised Land.

Come to the Table: What's your name?

"Then the king [David] said, "Is there not still someone of the house of Saul, to whom I may show the kindness of God?" And Ziba said to the king, "There is still a son of Jonathan who is lame in his feet" (2 Samuel 9:3).

We all have a name. You know, that one you use when completing your nametag, filling out an application, or purchasing items online. While it might be required for social security purposes, many of us know ourselves by other names. For despite having asserted on the playground, *"Sticks and stones may break my bones, but words will never hurt me,"* we've discovered later in life they, in fact, did. "I'm dumb." "I'm ugly." "I'm a poor speaker." "I'm weak." "I'm clumsy." I'm fat." "I'm a failure." "I'm a loser." "I'm _____." If you think and speak a new name about yourself, then you've renamed yourself. This is how you actually identify, define, and label who you really believe you are. Much like Ziba, who described the unnamed person David wanted to show the *"kindness of God"* to. The one who was merely known as he who was *"lame in his feet."*

In Christ, you have a new name. Most likely, it is not the one given to you at birth, and definitely not any of the negative labels assigned to you by yourself or others. You are a child of the King. A son or daughter. Redeemed, adopted, forgiven, chosen, a temple of God, accepted, Christ's friend, complete in Him, united with the Lord, His workmanship, and given a spirit of power, love, and a sound mind. And so much more. This is who you really are, unlike the labels we've adopted over the years. For you are who God says you are.

No, he is not the one who is *"lame in his feet."* He is Mephibosheth, the one God showed kindness to. An orphan adopted by both the King and the King of Kings.

Come to the Table: Called Out of Lo Debar

"So the king said to him, 'Where is he?' And Ziba said to the king, 'Indeed he is in the house of Machir the son of Ammiel, in Lo Debar.' Then King David sent and brought him out of the house of Machir the son of Ammiel, from Lo Debar" (2 Samuel 9:4-5).

While it seems incredibly harsh and cruel to our 21st-century senses, in David's day, it was very common for a new king to kill all the family members of the king they had deposed. As the only remaining relative of King Saul, the orphan Mephibosheth, when he received word King David wanted to see him, must have thought, "This is it. I'm a goner." I'm sure he must have thought he'd be safe in Lo Debar. Located in the wilderness east of the Jordan River, it was a town of forgotten people. Out in the wilderness, it was a place where the lost, the unskilled, the uneducated, and the outcasts from society lived. The invisible one's others passed by. The ones disenfranchised and marginalized. An island of misfit toys.

The name Lo Debar itself means *not having*, *no pasture*, or *no word*. The people who lived there lacked communication with the outside world, and ongoing hopelessness was always on the menu. The Lo Debar folks were lonely and isolated…. out of the mainstream of society. How easy for the citizens of Lo Debar to develop what one might call *Lo Debar thinking*. "Nothing will ever change for me." "I'm stuck here with no escape." "My problems are so big." "My circumstances are overwhelming." "I'm forgotten, and no one cares."

But King David *"brought him out"* to show him God's kindness. In an instant, everything changed for Mephibosheth. Like what God in Christ did for us. No matter how hopeless a situation you might find yourself in today, no matter the labels others may have given you, no matter the discouragement or setbacks you've endured, no matter the shame you've carried – if the Lord can do it for a forgotten man with lame feet in a vast wilderness isolated from any help – He can and will do it for you and me!

Come to the Table: A Seat Reserved for You

"Now when Mephibosheth the son of Jonathan, the son of Saul, had come to David, he fell on his face and prostrated himself…. So David said to him, "Do not fear, for I will restore to you all the land of Saul your grandfather; and you shall eat bread at my table continually" (2 Samuel 9:6-7).

David reached out to King Saul's last remaining relative. Expecting death, Mephibosheth received God's kindness. He brought nothing to the table except his lame feet. David wanted him just as he was—no strings attached, no cleanup necessary. Here you go, Meph—come to my table and spend the rest of your life as the king's son!

How familiar this sounds. Didn't we all once live in Lo Debar? We didn't go looking for Jesus, but He came looking for us. Lame in our feet, we too brought nothing to the table. Dead, hopeless, and lost, and then God demonstrated *"His own love towards us, in that while we were still sinners, Christ died for us"* (Romans 5:8). We were brought into the King's home and given all the rights and privileges of sitting at His table as a son or daughter. Having been dropped, damaged, and wounded by life, we are now always welcome at the table of the Lord. A permanent seat – a new home and a new life. As the redeemed, our Father no longer sees us according to our inadequacies, deficiencies, or problems. He treats us as His children, fully accepted in His love and grace.

So, let's abandon the Lo Debar thinking of our past. Instead, may we be constantly overwhelmed by the Father's goodness, kindness, love, beauty, and splendor rather than our circumstances, struggles, issues, or needs. Let's allow God's goodness to change how we think and act. This is God's mission for us: To look to His Word for guidance, counsel, wisdom, truth, and answers for all of life. To overcome darkness through the renewing of our minds, carrying the truth of His Word, the presence of the Holy Spirit, and the kindness of God wherever we go.

Flourishing Friendships: Genuine Listening

"Set a guard, O Lord, over my mouth; keep watch over the door of my lips"
(Psalm 141:3).

We live in an age of constant and immediate communication—quickly approaching the breaking point of TMI. We are a distracted people, drinking the water of information through a digital fire hose. In this distracted age, the raw material of conversation—genuine listening—has developed into a rare commodity. And yet, it is the greatest of gifts, because we are giving the person our most valuable asset: our attention. Here are some practical helps so we may *"... be swift to hear, slow to speak..."*:

1. **Listen, don't talk** – Listen to understand vs. waiting for an opening to respond. It's not about you. If they're talking about trouble in their job, don't tell them how much trouble you're having at work. If they're telling you about their vacation, don't change the subject and start talking about your vacation. *"Let each of you look out not only for his own interests, but the interests of others"* (Philippians 2:4).
2. **Don't finish the other person's sentence** – Although prolonged thinking and slow talking can activate impatience, show respect and honor to the speaker by not abruptly jumping in.
3. **Your body language says a lot** – Look the other person in the eye and lean forward. Practice "heart to heart," with your heart facing their heart (vs. the TV or computer). Show honor by not checking your phone or looking at the clock. The most important person in the world is the person in front of you.
4. **Notice the little things** – Listen for details and pick up on them later. For example: "You mentioned you spent a lot of time as a child at your grandmother's. What kind of relationship did you have with her?"
5. **Be a friend and not a judge** – For you problem solvers out there, resist the temptation to give advice. Unless, of course, they are actually asking you for it.
6. **Be aware of how much you are talking** – Everyone has 3.6 blind spots. Lack of self-awareness is a huge issue for most of us. Let's not dominate the conversation.

Active, engaged listening, done to understand, may be the most significant attribute of a loving friendship—an attribute our listening Father displays towards us in giving each of His beloved children His undivided attention.

Flourishing Friendships: He Listens

"Then those who feared the Lord, spoke with one another. The Lord paid attention and heard them, and a book of remembrance was written before Him of those who feared the Lord and esteemed His name" (Malachi 3:16).

In this last book of the Old Testament, we read about another book—a book remembering those who held God in awe and worshiped Him as the Lord Almighty. These believers met together not to complain but to encourage and build one another up. They spoke about the Lord and weren't afraid of Him hearing what they had to say. How incredible to think the Lord hears our edifying conversations and records our names in this heavenly book.

As believers in Jesus, God calls us to steward our relationships because we are part of His kingdom, His plans, and His purposes. We serve a Good King who promises to redeem every act prompted by faith. He never forces compliance, but He rewards those who diligently seek Him. He never shames us for our weakness, but He shines brightly through the low places of our lives. He never bullies us into surrender, but He lovingly dares us to trust Him. Now, friends of Jesus, He confides in us with insight as we seek Him, speaks to us through His living Word, and breathes life in us through His Holy Spirit. He establishes us in His goodness and mercy, sustaining us through His power and grace. Once orphans, now we are heirs. Once separated, now we are friends.

So scroll through your contacts and prayerfully consider who you might cultivate a friendship with. Move out of your comfort zone, lean in, and listen to their stories as the Lord does to yours. Be curious, ask questions, and pray with them before you depart. Let's constantly be reminding one another just how great our God is!

I Can Fix It

"Trust in the Lord with all your heart, and lean not on your own understanding" (Proverbs 3:5).

I'm no scientist, but as I understand it in layman's terms, the second law of thermodynamics states a fundamental yet simple truth about the universe: Entropy always increases with time. Everything breaks down from complex to simple. From life and order…. to death and disorder. Isn't that lovely? Pretty gloomy endgame, I'd say. Now, what I've discovered, is that those who can temporarily stem the tide of entropy (AKA those good at fixing things and problem-solving) are highly esteemed and regarded in society. At work, in the community, and in the home. And it's not just *things* that are always breaking down. People break down too! As a result, our world places great value and spends exorbitant amounts on people and products that can temporarily reverse the inevitable. From marketplace leaders who can solve the latest organizational problems to DIY experts who can fix leaky roofs to the makers of lotions and potions who can momentarily reverse the aging process. As long as there is entropy, there will always be a high demand for the problem-solvers and fixers of life.

As one who naturally defaults to wanting to fix everything impacted by entropy, I've grown to see a universal principle to be true: *Your greatest strength is your greatest weakness.* Having had many pats on the back for solving the latest problem or thing, it's difficult to see how this could ever be a weakness. Surely that which reverses entropy and is rewarded by the world would always be a good thing, right? Well, not necessarily. Especially when it comes to trusting and waiting upon the Lord. We problem solvers are apt to quickly fix the latest issue or problem, and to do so without prayer. Without a dependency or reliance upon the God of order, the One who *"is before all things, and in Him all things hold together"* (Colossians 1:17).

So to all my fellow fixers and problem-solvers: Keep doing what you do. Our entropic world needs you! And as you do, always be leaning on the Lord in prayer, with a holy surrender, trust, and dependence upon Him as your daily way of life. Then, and only then, will your labor not be in vain, for *"Unless the Lord builds the house, they labor in vain who build it"* (Psalm 127:1).

Little By Little

"And the Lord your God will drive out those nations before you little by little; you will be unable to destroy them at once, lest the beasts of the field become too numerous for you" (Deuteronomy 7:22).

We don't like *"little by little."* We like *really big all at once right now*. Especially when it comes to answered prayer and deliverance from trials. Having been fed a steady diet of Hollywood superheroes swooping in and saving the day in the blink of an eye, this *"little by little"* seems mundane and underwhelming. If we're completely honest, don't we all want *really big all at once right now* to happen for all our most vexing problems and difficult trials? Complete deliverance..... immediately. As in today. No? Then how about tomorrow? At the latest, please. But alas, we soon discover in life these immediate fixes are not the norm. Gradual is.

Why is that? The Israelites had seen God act instantly: the parting of the Red Sea, the manna, the quail, the water from a rock. They knew God could do the miraculous at any moment. And so do we. We've read our Bibles, we've had our experiences, and we've heard the stories of others. So, in addition to the *"beasts of the field"* mentioned above, why does God choose gradual over sudden for the bulk of life? We see the clues throughout chapters 7 and 8 of Deuteronomy:

- **To build faith (vs. fear):** *"You shall not be terrified of them; for the Lord your God, the great and awesome God, is among you"* (Deut. 7:21). Over time, trust in God increases our faith.
- **To build humility (vs. pride):** *"…. the Lord your God led you all the way these forty years in the wilderness, to humble you and test you"* (Deut. 8:2). Over time, the crucible of life humbles us.
- **To build remembrance (vs. forgetfulness):** *"Beware you do not forget…. you shall remember the Lord your God, for it is He who gives you power to get wealth"* (Deut. 8:11, 18). Over time, His ongoing faithful hand imprints and hardcodes our memory.

Yes, God could certainly change your circumstances instantly without your cooperation or participation. And sometimes He does. But ultimately, His glory and your conformity into Christ will always be His chief priority for us…. and in us. And that takes time.

Carpe Diem

"Better to go to the house of mourning than to the house of feasting, for that is the end of all men; and the living will take it to heart" (Ecclesiastes 7:2).

Charles Hummell wrote a short book in 1967 called *The Tyranny of the Urgent.* In it, he describes the constant tension between the things that are urgent versus the things that are important. "Your greatest danger is letting the urgent things crowd out the important things." Tasks, errands, work, and the demands of life. The pressing matters of the day often push away the things that truly matter. Accomplishing our to-do list while leaving the significant and eternal for another day. A day that, for many, never comes.

In his book *The Road to Character*, David Brooks distinguishes between "resume virtues" and "eulogy virtues." Resume virtues are what *we* talk about while still alive – our education, experience, accomplishments, and achievements in life. Eulogy virtues, on the other hand, are what *others* talk about after we're dead – our character, love, charity, and influence we had on the lives we leave behind.

Both writers point to the same principle: Live life by beginning with the end. And so, here's the big spoiler alert: You will die. Ponce DeLeon, unfortunately, never did find that fountain of youth he was looking for. Yes, despite the best efforts of the global anti-aging market, estimated to be worth $83.2 billion by 2027, death awaits us all. So then, how shall we live? Will we distract ourselves from the inevitable by amusing ourselves with the latest trivial pursuits, or will we prioritize investing in the two things that last forever: The Word of God and people?

Go to the house of mourning and live a life well lived. Love the Lord with all your heart, soul, mind, and strength, and invest your life in the people who will cry at your funeral.

Sin in the Camp

"Hidden among you, O Israel, are things set apart for the Lord. You will never defeat your enemies until you remove these things from among you"
(Joshua 7:13 NLT).

As a child of God, you have joined a family destined for victory. We, the church, who have received an *"abundance of grace"* and the *"gift of righteousness will reign in life through the One, Jesus Christ"* (Romans 5:17). Through Christ, we *will* reign in life, and through Christ, we *will* live in victory: *"But thanks be to God, who gives us the victory through our Lord Jesus Christ"* (1 Corinthians 15:57). Reigning victoriously in life, *"we are more than conquerors through Him who loved us"* (Romans 8:37). All this is ours because He reigns victoriously as our Supreme Conqueror, *"And Jesus came and spoke to them, saying, 'All authority has been given to Me in heaven and on earth'"* (Matthew 28:18).

That said, why might we feel the opposite? Destined for victory, why might we feel defeated? There could be many reasons, but one in particular is highlighted in Scripture: The potential of hidden sin. Not that which is unknown to you but one you know well. The big "E" on your own personal eye chart. Something you've chosen to hide. By design. Blatant and egregious behavior you've chosen to keep in the dark. Like Achan, who chose to hide the gold and silver in his tent, leading to Israel's defeat at Ai (Joshua 7:4-21). Or Ananias and Sapphira, who lied about the amount of their sale of land to both the Holy Spirit and the apostles (Acts 5:1-11). Two instances where sin attempted to hijack the promised victory. Israel, who was destined to conquer the promised land. And the church, destined for victory in advancing Christ's kingdom here on earth. The rule and reign of Christ our King will never be thwarted. And He will make sure of that.

Integrity is what we do when nobody is watching. As believers, let's walk in the light as He is in the light, for He indeed is watching and sees. Don't wait until you are caught. Confess and repent now instead. *"If we confess our sins, he is faithful and just to forgive us our sins and cleanse us from all unrighteousness"* (1 John 1:9). The sooner we do, the sooner we will begin to walk in and experience the promised victory He's given to each of us, *"For all the promises of God in Him are Yes, and in Him Amen, to the glory of God through us* (2 Corinthians 1:20).

Life Upon Life: The Story of Ruth

"But Ruth said: Entreat me not to leave you, or to turn back from following after you; for wherever you, I will go; and wherever you lodge, I will lodge; your people shall be my people, and your God, my God" (Ruth 1:16).

The book of Ruth occurs during the time of the Judges in Israel. At a time when there was no king in Israel, but *"everyone did what was right in his own eyes"* (Judges 17:6). At one of the lowest points in the nation's history – a time of division, cruelty, and apostasy – the man Elimelech, his wife Naomi, and their two sons flee to Moab to escape famine and death. Planning to stay temporarily, they remain for ten years. Their two sons marry, and then the unthinkable happens. Elimelech dies, as do Naomi's two sons, leaving Naomi with her two daughters-in-law, Ruth and Orpah. Just imagine the three of them sitting at the kitchen table, together but alone… the bonds that had held them seemingly gone… each woman wilting under her loss. What will I do? What happens next? How will I survive, pick up the pieces, and move forward?

Leaving Moab behind, the trio decides to journey to Israel. Turning back, we never know what happened to Orpah, but Naomi and Ruth press on to the town of Bethlehem. Upon their arrival, Naomi says to the townspeople, *"Do not call me Naomi (sweetness); call me Mara (bitter), for the Almighty has caused me great grief and bitterness"* (Ruth 1:20). Transparent about her bitterness, Naomi was very open about how she felt and how she was navigating the losses in her life. What a good reminder. We all deal with our emotions, but what we do with them determines our trajectory in life.

Naomi took her broken heart and her broken life and replanted herself back in the land of the Lord's people. She removed herself from the land of the Moabites and their idolatrous worship of the false god Chemosh. Naomi knew she would find care, comfort, grace, and love among the people of God. She understood the significance of organic connection to the people of God, or as we say today – the Body of Christ. Just as *"apart from Me [Jesus] you can do nothing"* (John 15:5), so apart from the Body, each member cannot function as God intended, for an index finger severed and detached from the body is incapable of pointing to a single thing. In our pain and loss, we need the Living God and God's people, which Naomi and Ruth understood deeply.

Life Upon Life: The Grace of our God

"So Naomi returned, and Ruth the Moabitess her daughter-in-law with her, who returned from the country of Moab. Now they came to Bethlehem at the beginning of the barley harvest" (Ruth 1:22).

Everything in and around her presented obstacles to her faith, yet Ruth trusted in and believed in the God of Israel. Her Moabite upbringing with their worship of Chemosh, coupled with the loss of her husband, could have made her very bitter and angry towards Naomi's God, but instead, she embraced Him. With the town stirred with Naomi's return and the Moabite woman she brought with her, it was time for the barley harvest and the entrance of the third character in this story: Boaz, whose name means "in him is strength."

As a woman, a poor widow, and a foreigner in the land, Ruth had no claims on anyone – she was on the lowest rung of the social ladder in that day. So she sets out to glean in the fields, the Old Testament equivalent of our welfare system. Boaz, the farmer in our story, would leave behind the leftovers of the harvest, enabling the poor and needy to come behind and glean what they could to survive. Ruth just so happens to glean in the field of Boaz (Ruth 2:3), and he quickly spots this stranger in his field (Ruth 2:5). Upon learning it's Ruth, Boaz gives her a beautiful blessing, *"May the Lord reward you for what you have done... and may you receive a full reward from the Lord God of Israel, under whose wings you have come for refuge"* (Ruth 2:12).

Boaz was kind to the most lowly. He didn't owe Ruth anything, but he gave her everything. The picture of Boaz's plentiful harvest was a sign of God's covenantal blessing on Boaz, and Boaz's abundant generosity to Ruth as she gleans in his field (Ruth 2:15-23) reveals his cheerful desire to leave a large part of his harvest for the poor and the sojourner. This is the heart of our God. As a foreshadowing of Christ, Boaz wields strength and power to serve and bless others. May we also, poor and needy like Ruth, flee to Jesus and find our refuge under His wings, *"He will cover you with His feathers, and under His wings you will find refuge; His faithfulness will be your shield and rampart"* (Psalm 91:4).

Life Upon Life:
Big Doors Swing on Small Hinges

"So Boaz took Ruth and she became his wife… and she bore a son. And they called his name Obed. He is the father of Jesse, the father of David" (Ruth 4:13, 17).

The book of Ruth begins with tremendous sadness but culminates with great joy. Boaz and Ruth marry in the little town of Bethlehem and have a baby boy, Obed, who will become the grandfather of King David, from whose line the Lord Jesus Christ will be born. As a type and shadow of Christ, Boaz was God's provision for Ruth, just as Jesus is God's provision for us.

Throughout Ruth, we see Boaz as a foreshadowing of Jesus and His relationship with His bride, the church. In chapters 2 and 3, Boaz took the initiative to reach out to Ruth first; he spoke kindly to her; he promised to protect Ruth and provide for her needs, and then he encouraged her and blessed her. In this we see the beauty of how God speaks to us in Christ through His Word. Like Boaz, He assures us (3:8-10) and accepts us (3:10-14). And in chapter 4, we learn Boaz is the family's kinsman redeemer. In Mosaic Law, a kinsman redeemer is a male relative with the privilege and responsibility to act on behalf of a relative in trouble, danger, or need. The Hebrew word for it, *go el,* means "one who delivers or rescues or redeems property." What an apt description of our Lord and Savior. As our Kinsman Redeemer, Jesus has bought us for Himself, made us His beloved bride, and blessed us to a thousand generations.

The story of Ruth shows there are no insignificant people in God's plan. Big doors swing on small hinges! He takes the despised and rejected, the lowly and needy, and He binds them to Christ. What looks messy and meaningless to us, from God's perspective, is an intentional and precise way He is working to establish His Kingdom. If God includes foreigners, illegitimate children, and prostitutes in the family tree of Jesus (Matthew 1:1-17), He will include you too. No matter your background, issues, start in life, or current status – you are significant to God's plan of redemption. You may feel you have nothing to offer, but that is a lie straight from the pit. Just look at Ruth! Broken and displaced, from a "persona non grata" people group, God used her to write His redemption story. In the same way, your redemptive story is a message your world desperately needs to hear too.

The Faith of Caleb

"Then Caleb quieted the people before Moses, and said, 'Let us go up at once and take possession, for we are well able to overcome it... the Lord is with us. Do not fear them'" (Numbers 13:30; 14:9).

Sent in by Moses, the spies operated a covert reconnaissance mission of the promised land for the children of Israel. Upon their return, these twelve men had reached a common consensus: The land *"truly flows with milk and honey"* (Numbers 13:27). But that's as far as it went. Ten spies came to one conclusion, and Joshua and Caleb came to another. For the ten, all they saw were *"the people who are strong, the cities fortified and very large, and the descendants of Anak... the giants"* (Joshua 13:28, 33). All Joshua and Caleb saw was their God.

This, then, is the crux of life: What do we see? Or, more accurately, Whom do we see? Will we walk by faith, or will we walk by sight (2 Corinthians 5:7)? The one path leads to victory, the other to defeat and wandering confusion. Will we take God at His Word, believing and trusting in Him, or will our final conclusions about any matter in life be driven by our eyes, conventional wisdom, or fear? As we've mentioned before, your faith is *"much more precious than gold"* (1 Peter 1:7), so we now know and understand His value system. He values what Joshua and Caleb had, to the point where God told Moses, *"My servant Caleb, because he has a different spirit in him and has followed Me fully, I will bring into the land where he went, and his descendants shall inherit it"* (Numbers 14:24). Don't we want to be different too?

Unlike any other book ever written, *"the word of God is living and powerful and sharper than any two-edged sword"* (Hebrews 4:12), pointing us to Jesus, the One to whom *"All authority has been given"* (Matthew 28:18). So let's *"not become sluggish, but imitate those who through faith and patience inherit the promises"* (Hebrews 6:12). Let's be different and imitate Caleb.

The Patience of Caleb

"The Lord has kept me [Caleb] alive, as He said, these forty-five years, ever since the Lord spoke this word to Moses while Israel wandered in the wilderness; and now here I am eighty-five years old" (Joshua 14:10).

Forty-five years is a long time to wait. I find forty-five days to be a long time. And depending on the circumstance (like getting the test results back), forty-five hours may seem like an eternity. To compound matters, Caleb wasn't at fault! *They* were the problem. The other ten spies……and the frightened children of Israel aligned behind them. What a disheartening experience it must have been to get the word you'll have to wait for decades for something you were personally innocent of. Talk about *guilty by association*.

History will never record our culture as being too patient. Rather, quite the opposite. In a microwave society that expects same-day delivery, we are easily frazzled when our download is delayed by a minute or two. As I type this, I am on hold with our cell phone provider as they attempt to resolve a problem they created. We're at twenty-four minutes and fifty-three seconds, but who's counting? I'm patiently waiting, or am I? I find an inner agitation just below the surface. But I know suppression and a fake smile isn't the answer. True patience is.

I'd like to offer two considerations for an increase in patience. First, patience is a by-product. Like a healthy tree producing good fruit is a by-product of its health (Matthew 7:17). This is why patience is listed as a fruit of the Spirit (Galatians 5:22). It comes by grace through faith. Faith in God produces the patience of God. Second, to become a more patient person, the time to build those "muscles" is *not* when we need to use them. If I've been asked to help move a piano, the time to develop the strength to be a valuable contributor is *not* in the moment the move occurs. The building of those muscles needs to occur *before* the move. *"Looking unto Jesus, the author and finisher of our faith"* (Hebrews 12:20), trusting in Him and His promises, believing He is *always* in providential control of *all* circumstances in my life. Long before I've chosen the line at Safeway that isn't moving.

And for those of you on the edge of your seat regarding the cell phone saga, the story had a happy ending. At the seventy-three-minute mark. *"But for You, O Lord, do I wait; it is You, O Lord, who will answer"* (Psalm 38:15).

The Boldness of Caleb

"Now therefore, give me this mountain of which the Lord spoke in that day; for you heard in that day how the Anakim were there... it may be that the Lord will be with me, and I shall be able to drive them out as the Lord said" (Joshua 14:12).

At eighty-five years of age, Caleb wanted his mountain. The mountain the Lord said he could have forty-five years earlier. He had patiently waited all those years, and now he wanted it. Even though, using conventional wisdom, he had two strikes against him. He was eighty-five, and the giants were still there. But no problem for Caleb. *"As yet I am as strong this day as on the day that Moses sent me; just as my strength was then, so now is my strength for war"* (Joshua 14:11). And even though the giants (AKA the Anakim) were still there, after Joshua blessed him and said he could have it, the eighty-five-year-old Caleb led the charge, and the land of Hebron became his, the Bible says, *"because he wholly followed the Lord God of Israel"* (Joshua 14:14).

Two takeaways from this portion of Caleb's story. First, *"You do not have because you do not ask God"* (James 4:2). We need to be people who are constantly asking of God in alignment with His Word. Note verse 12 above: *".....as the Lord said".* If you are in Christ, then all the promises in His Word are yes and amen. They are for you. If you read it, He has said it, and now He wants you to ask Him for it. And note how the fruit didn't fall far from the tree with Caleb. His daughter Othniel had the same bold spirit, *"Caleb said to her, 'What do you wish?' She answered, 'Give me a blessing; since you have given me land in the South, give me also springs of water.' So he gave her the upper springs and the lower springs"* (Joshua 15:18-19). We do not have because we do not ask.

Second, be bold like Caleb. Despite your best efforts doing P90X or CrossFit, you probably won't possess forty-year-old strength at eighty-five, but that's ok. You still can be just as bold regardless of age. Our sympathetic High Priest has gone before us, so He wants us to *"come boldly to the throne of grace, that we may obtain mercy and find grace to help in time of need"* (Hebrews 4:16). Every moment of every day is our time of need, so let's be a people boldly and persistently asking for the mountains He has promised to give us.

The Dimensions of Praise

*"Every day I will bless You, and I will praise Your name forever and ever.
Great is the Lord, and greatly to be praised;
and His greatness is unsearchable" (Psalm 145:2-3).*

Hebrew is the language of the Old Testament. In this language, the people of God used three different words for the word *praise* in their worship of Him. Let's examine these three words in the Psalms and how they might deepen our understanding of our praise and worship of the Lord:

Towdah – *To extend our hands in faith, adoration, and thanksgiving.* Hands are raised in a receiving posture, reaching out in trust and surrender as we look up to God, acknowledging Him as our Source. It means a sacrifice of praise for things not yet received. When we engage in this expression, when we raise our hands heavenward, we are pointing to the very place of our ultimate hope. *"Whoever offers praise [towdah] glorifies Me; and to him who orders his conduct aright, I will show the salvation of God"* (Psalm 50:23).

Barak – *A song of praise springing from thanksgiving.* It's the idea of falling to your knees in adoration and gratitude. This word expresses humility and embodies the notion of kneeling before God, blessing and adoring Him, and recognizing our position in relation to Him. It's a word used two hundred eighty-nine times in the Psalms, and on each occurrence, it's used to describe worshippers falling on their faces before God in reverence, adoration, and thanks. *"Praise [barak] the Lord, my soul; all my inmost being, praise His holy name. Praise [barak] the Lord, my soul, and forget not all His benefits...praise [barak] the Lord, all His works everywhere in His dominion"* (Psalm 103:1-2, 22).

Tehillah – *A hymn, a song of praise, or a new, spontaneous song.* Tehillah is a word used fifty-seven times in the Bible, with over half of those occurrences found in the Psalms. Songs of tehillah flow from the depths of intimacy with God. Have you ever found yourself so overcome with His goodness in your personal story that you can't help but sing to Him? *"But you are holy, enthroned in the praises [tehillah] of Israel"* (Psalm 22:3). The Lord steps from His heavenly courts and takes residency among the congregation. He meets us in our rejoicing and praise.

Who Did It?

"And I sent terror ahead of you to drive out the two kings of the Amorites. It was not your swords or bows that brought you the victory" (Joshua 24:12).

In the 1965 movie *Shenandoah,* Jimmy Stewart plays Charlie Anderson, a Virginian father of a large family living during the outbreak of the Civil War. Having promised his dying wife he would raise their seven children as good Christians, Charlie reluctantly takes them to church, and here offers a rather interesting prayer of "thanksgiving" around their abundantly filled table:

"Lord, we cleared this land. We plowed it, sowed it, and harvested it. We cooked the harvest. It wouldn't be here, we wouldn't be eatin' it if we hadn't done it all ourselves. We worked dog-bone hard for every crumb and morsel, but we thank you just the same anyway, Lord, for this food we're about to eat. Amen."

It seems Charlie thought the Lord didn't do much of anything regarding the food they were about to enjoy. He obviously recognized the human element of their food chain, but not the divine. To Charlie, God seemed a mere peripheral spectator. So, how should we consider the intersection of our labors and God?

In the above verse from Joshua, the Israelites undoubtedly spent much effort wielding their swords and bows. But that's not what brought them victory. And while many beautiful homes have been built by those who don't believe, God says, *"Unless the Lord builds the house, its builders labor in vain"* (Psalm 127:1). Even Paul, who in the same letter said, *"I worked harder than all of them"* (1 Corinthians 15:10), recognized his limitations and complete dependency upon His grace, *"I planted, Apollos watered, but God gave the increase"* (1 Corinthians 3:6).

Someday, we'll all stand before Him and have eternal clarity. It was all from God: Our ability to work, and the fruits of that labor. *"Always give yourselves fully to the work of the Lord, because you know that your labor in the Lord is not in vain"* (1 Corinthians 15:58). In Christ, even a cup of cold water has great eternal value and significance. As a believer, all your efforts have eternal meaning and purpose, seeing Him as the fount of it all.

Contrary to Charlie's prayer, *"Every good and perfect gift is from above, coming from the Father of lights"* (James 1:17). It's all from Him and for Him, because *"Apart from Me, you can do nothing"* (John 15:5).

No One Will Ever Know

"There is a way that seems right to a man, but its end is the way of death"
(Proverbs 16:25).

David thought he had everyone fooled. Having slept with another man's wife and having discovered she was pregnant, he then came up with a plan to murder her soldier husband while the army of Israel was at war (1 Samuel 11). *No one will ever know*, so David must have thought, until the prophet Nathan confronted him and declared, *"You are the man!"* (2 Samuel 12:7). And their baby would die soon thereafter.

Shimei once cursed that very same David when it appeared David would lose his kingdom to his son Absalom (2 Samuel 16:5-14). Years later, as punishment, Solomon told Shimei he could live but must remain in Jerusalem for the rest of his life and never leave upon penalty of death (1 Kings 2:36-37). Three years later, Shimei quietly slipped out of Jerusalem and traveled to the city of Gath to find his two lost slaves and quickly returned to the city (1 Kings 2:39-46). *Surely the king has forgotten or is busied with many other far more important matters,* he must have thought. *He'll never know.* But know he did, and King Solomon kept his word to Shimei.

Ananias and Sapphira were a couple who sold land, kept some of the profit, and then gave the remaining balance to the apostles under the guise that it was the full amount (Acts 5). Seemed to be the perfect plot, being able to keep some money while receiving the desired praise of the church community. *No one will ever know*. But the Holy Spirit knew, and in the end, they *"fell down and breathed his (her) last"* (Acts 5:5,10).

Supreme Court Justice Louis Brandeis once said, *"Sunlight is said to be the best disinfectant."* In life, there are no secrets. Sure, we might fool a person or two, but in the end, nobody fools Him. So let's walk accordingly, in the light as He is in the light. Where life is: *"I am the Way, the Truth, and the Life"* (John 14:6). Where Jesus is.

> *"Therefore judge nothing before the time, until the Lord comes, who will both bring to light the hidden things of darkness and reveal the counsels of the hearts. Then each one's praise will come from God"*
> (1 Corinthians 4:5).

A Long Obedience in the Same Direction

"But the Israelites encouraged each other and took their positions again at the same place they had fought the previous day" (Judges 20:22).

At the end of the book of Judges, we're told of a heinous sin and a horrific series of events culminating in a civil war and the near destruction of the tribe of Benjamin. At the start and throughout the war, the tribes of Israel kept inquiring of the Lord if they should attack Benjamin. The first two times, the Lord told them to do so. And both times, the ten tribes were soundly defeated by Benjamin. In fact, the above verse falls right in between their first and second defeat. Finally, only on the third inquiry did the Lord tell them to go once again, and in doing so, He would give them the victory.

Maybe you've felt directed by the Lord to a particular place, person, or position in life. A place you've moved to, a job you've taken, a church you've joined, or a person you're in a relationship with. If we're honest, don't we expect and anticipate only happiness, bliss, victory, and joy on the other side of our obedience to His direction? But what if, on the other side, we experience just the opposite? What if, on the other side, we encounter adversity, meet opposition, and face defeat? Does that necessarily mean we got it wrong? Not necessarily. There are times we must do precisely what the Israelites did after being soundly defeated the day before: Encourage one another, take up our positions once again, and do so in the exact same place where we fought and lost the day before. For while we do not know what the new day will bring, we do know His mercy and compassion await us. For as Jeremiah declared amidst his apparent defeats:

> *"This I recall to my mind, therefore I have hope. Through the Lord's mercies we are not consumed, because His compassions fail not. They are new every morning; great is your faithfulness. 'The Lord is my portion,' says my soul, 'Therefore I hope in Him!'" (Lamentations 3:21-24).*

Not One Word

"Not a word failed of any good thing which the Lord had spoken to the house of Israel. All came to pass" (Joshua 21:45).

If you've ever recorded a sporting event to watch later in the day, are in the middle of reading a page-turning book, or are planning to see a popular action movie, aren't you grateful when someone issues a spoiler alert? We all want to be kept in suspense until we can find out, on our own, how the story ends. For without a doubt, someone with complete knowledge has an advantage over those who don't. They possess hindsight, and with it comes the benefit of 20/20 vision.

The above verse from Joshua is the conclusion of God's people inheriting the promised land. What began in Exodus 3 with the Lord telling Moses at the burning bush, *"I have come down to deliver them out of the hand of the Egyptians, and bring them up from the land to a good and large land, to a land flowing with milk and honey... "* (Exodus 3:8), now finds its conclusion one hundred and fifty-four chapters later in Joshua, *"So the Lord gave to Israel all the land of which He had sworn to give to their fathers, and they took possession of it and dwelt in it"* (Joshua 21:43). Having the benefit of hindsight, Joshua could conclude it all came to pass. God was faithful, His word was true, and He delivered on all His promises. Every. Single. One.

So here's your spoiler alert (but please keep reading): With similar clarity, what Joshua was able to conclude with the benefit of hindsight, you too will be able to conclude about your own life. God has written the final chapter of your story, and while it has not yet been experienced by you, He can be trusted for the ending. What was true for Israel and their experience with God, will be true for you too. Having 20/20 vision, you'll look back and see that it all came to pass. All His promises. Every. Single. One.

Stay Humble

*"... Saul went to Carmel, and indeed, he set up a
monument for himself..."* (1 Samuel 15:12).

King Saul is a fascinating study of what *not* to do when fame, fortune, and/or power come your way. Having begun with humility when tapped to be the first King of Israel – *"Am I not a Benjamite, of the smallest of the tribes of Israel, and my family the least of all the families of the tribe of Benjamin?"* (1 Samuel 9:21) – ended with him building a monument to himself. How could this be? How did he progress from apparent humility to apparent pride? From being accepted by God *("This one shall reign over my people")* to being rejected by Him *("the Lord has rejected you from being king over Israel")*? For *"God resists the proud, but gives grace to the humble"* (1 Peter 5:5). And don't we all want and need more grace in our lives?

One contributing factor from the life of King Saul seems to be his incessant love for the praise of man. And his incessant fear of them. The applause, praise, and bright lights of success are prone to activate a desire for more of the same. They are very addictive. Only after Samuel pressed Saul regarding his rebellion, stubbornness, and rejection of God did Saul finally concede why he did what he did, *"Then Saul said to Samuel, "I have sinned, for I have transgressed the commandment of the Lord and your words, because I feared the people and obeyed their voice"* (1 Samuel 15:24). In the end, Saul succumbed to the public opinion polls and not to God and His Word.

In contrast, we have Jesus. As his popularity began to grow, He did just the opposite. *"But Jesus would not entrust Himself to them, for He knew all people. He did not need any testimony about mankind, for he knew what was in each person"* (John 2:24-25). He knew one day they would be shouting *"Hosanna!"* and a few days later, *"Crucify Him!"*. The praise of man is so fickle; let's entrust ourselves to Him alone and *"... make it our aim... to be well pleasing to Him"* (2 Corinthians 5:9).

From the hymn *When I Survey the Wondrous Cross*:

*Forbid it, Lord, that I should boast, save in the death of Christ, my God;
All the vain things that charm me most, I sacrifice them to His blood.*

*Were the whole realm of nature mine, that were a present far too small:
Love so amazing, so divine, demands my soul, my life, my all.*

So Many Voices!

*"Forever; O Lord, Your word is settled in heaven.
I will never forget your precepts, for by them You have given me life"
(Psalm 119:89, 93).*

What a noisy world we live in. Blogs, memes, email, text, networks, webinars, influencers, images, eBooks, chats, newsletters, channels, videos, sites, reels, forums, podcasts etc., etc. How in the world does one sort out what to take in and what to reject? In other words, what is our signal, and what is our noise? A *signal* being the life-giving communication and information we desperately need, and the *noise* being the irrelevant static and chaotic interference constantly attempting to drown out the signal of our lives. And unfortunately, the problem isn't just reserved for our eyes and ears. Some of the loudest voices we must contend with are those in our minds—some of the cruelest voices in all the world.

Here's where we can learn from a baby. About four months in, a baby placed in a room with many voices will turn their head toward their mother's voice. The baby can sort through all the noise to identify their signal. The one who is of utmost importance to them. We, too, like a baby, need to identify our signal. A voice that doesn't change. A voice that is for us and not against us. A voice we want to make louder so that it rises above the random and ever-changing din of the noise. A voice we constantly turn to despite the many who clamor for our attention. That *"still, small voice"* (1 Kings 19:12).

Just because a voice is loud doesn't make it right. So, in this noisy, opinionated world of ours, let's run to the voice of the One who alone is constant, faithful, and good. He is our Good Shepherd, and we *"the sheep hear his voice; and he calls his own sheep by name and leads them out. And when he brings out his own sheep, he goes before them; and the sheep follow him, for they know his voice"* (John 10:3-4). In the Bible, we find our signal, *"For the word of God is living and powerful and sharper than any two-edged sword"* (Hebrews 4:12).

Let's turn our heads to His Word and live!

The End

"Whom do I have in heaven but You?
And with You, I desire nothing on earth" (Psalm 73:25).

Jeremiah 17:9 says, *"The heart is deceitful above all things, and desperately wicked; who can know it?"* Nowhere do we find this more evident than when we find ourselves in the middle of an overwhelming trial. Melted by the crucible of life, we cry out to God for deliverance. A marriage teetering on the brink of divorce. A diagnosis with a minimal survival rate. A wayward child. A major unplanned financial setback. And even something as trivial as two out in the bottom of the ninth inning in game seven. Whenever we find ourselves in desperate straits, it is quite appropriate to cry out to God for deliverance. The danger in doing so, as always, is our heart. It can so subtly and imperceptibly shift off Him and to the desired answer as our end game. Making Him a mere means to our ultimate end.

The Westminster Shorter Catechism is a summary of Christian doctrine written in 1646 by the Westminster Assembly, a group of English and Scottish theologians and laymen. The question is posed in it, "What is the chief end of man?" They answered, "Man's chief end is to glorify God and to enjoy Him forever." He is our end. Like Shadrach, Meshach, and Abed-Nego. Faced with the prospect of being burned alive in Nebuchadnezzar's fiery furnace, they declared,

> *"Our God whom we serve is able to deliver us from the burning fiery furnace, and he will deliver us from your hand. But if not, let it be known to you, O king, that we do not serve your gods, nor will we worship the gold image which you have set up"* (Daniel 3:17-18).

Whether in deliverance or death, they were only going to worship the one true God.

Whatever overwhelming trial you may be facing today, *"Seek the Lord while He may be found, call upon Him while He is near"* (Isaiah 55:6). In doing so, you will find Him there. Present. Listening. Attentive. Caring. Comforting. Consoling. And isn't that our chief end: Him and Him alone? *"Yea, though I walk through the valley of the shadow of death, I will fear no evil;* **for You are with me**; *Your rod and Your staff comfort me"* (Psalm 23:4).

End

*"If we find ourselves with a desire that
nothing in this world can satisfy,
the most probable explanation is
that we were made for another world."*

C. S. Lewis

Your Story Matters: Our Faith Response

"A prayer of Habakkuk the prophet, on Shigionoth. "Lord, I have heard of your fame; I stand in awe of your deeds, Lord. Renew them in our day, in our time make them known; in wrath remember mercy (Habakkuk 3:1-2).

What began in Chapter 1 as a frustrated complaint about God's silence, timing, and answer to his prayers, now ends in Chapter 3 with worship and adoration. The Hebrew term *Shigionoth* means a psalm with music expressive of strong emotions. This brief faith-filled prayer (song) declares a sense of trust and victory *("I stand in awe of your deeds")*, in stark contrast to the taunt song of doom in Chapter 2 and the confusion of Chapter 1. When Habakkuk got his eyes off the problem of an impending invasion and fixed his eyes on God, he could worship and approach God differently. For whatever we focus on, we empower and magnify. If we focus on the problem, then the problem grows, leaving us perplexed, unhappy, and overwhelmed. But if we focus on God and his greatness, all matters will pale in comparison. Daily deliberate worship acknowledges God's true worth – celebrating His worth-ship.

We also learn from this prayer how to pray in line with God's will. While earlier prayers asked God for things based on what he saw, now filled with adoration, Habakkuk prayer is based on who God is. *"Renew them in our day"* is a prayer for revival. To make new. To make alive. Habakkuk is no longer thinking about the coming invasion and trying to convince God to change His mind – instead, he is crying out to God for the revival and spiritual renewal of His people – no matter what happens, Habakkuk wants God's work to be done in the hearts and lives of His people. And not tomorrow. And not in some future generation: *"…in our day… in our time."*

"In wrath remember mercy." What an amazing request to leave with God – what an effective request – God is the God of mercy; so to pray for mercy, even in the day of His wrath, is to plead for that which is central to His heart and His character. *"Let us therefore come boldly to the throne of grace, that we may obtain mercy and find grace to help in time of need"* (Hebrews 4:16).

From the hymn *Great is Thy Faithfulness:*

Great is Thy Faithfulness! Great is Thy Faithfulness!
Morning by morning new mercies I see;
All I have needed Thy hand has provided.
Great is Thy faithfulness, Lord unto me!

Your Story Matters: His Story

*"You went forth for the salvation of Your people,
for salvation with Your Anointed" (Habakkuk 3:13).*

In Chapter 3:3-16, the transparent prophet begins to take us down the road of story and the Lord's redemption of His people. These verses recount God's glorious work in the world and in the lives of His people, leading to Habakkuk's grand declaration of worship and faith at the end of the chapter. The climatic verse in this passage is verse 13. Do the words *salvation* and *Anointed* conjure up a picture of a familiar Friend? Habakkuk 3:13 cross-references to Daniel 9:25 *"Know therefore and understand, that from the going forth of the command to restore and build Jerusalem until Messiah the Prince, there shall be 7 weeks….."* The word *Mashiach* in Hebrew is translated to Messiah or Anointed One, as both Daniel and Habakkuk point us to the greatest story ever told—God's story of His Son and our Savior, the Lord Jesus Christ.

Habakkuk knew the importance of story because stories reveal the faithfulness of God. He knew not only was God able to save His people, but He had promised to save them through the Anointed One. Do you see how the stories of the OT are critical to understanding the main story of the New? All the stories of the Old are a divine set-up. They all point to the fulfillment of the great story. Jesus the Messiah. Jesus the Christ. It's always, always, always about Jesus – my story and your story – He is the central character in it all.

This is why your story matters because your story points you and others to Yeshua Mashiach. Jesus Christ is the answer to life. To save us from sin, to provide us with a relationship with God, and to give us hope for the future. He is the Source of everything. He is your strength for the day, wisdom for the task, comfort for your soul, grace for your battle, provision for every need, understanding for each failure, and assistance for every encounter.

If you know Jesus, you have a story.

Your Story Matters: Your Testimony

"And with great power the apostles were giving testimony to the resurrection of the Lord Jesus, and abundant grace was upon them all" (Acts 4:33)

Stories have power. We all gravitate toward and love good stories. They hold us in rapt attention with their beginning, middle, and exciting end (except for the occasional cliffhanger with the dreaded *To Be Continued*). From birth, parents read stories to their children. As we grow, we pick up books and watch movies, documentaries, and TV shows that bring us to tears, laughter, or the edge of our seats. And when the sermon is a little dry, our ears and minds perk up when we hear, *"Let me tell you the story of..."*

The National Geographic Society stated:

"People remember how stories make them feel, and are more inspired to take action than if they just heard facts and figures. Stories are hardwired into our very biology. Our brains arrive filled with all the cognitive machinery needed to comprehend stories and share them with others."

While all stories have varying degrees of influence in our lives, there is no more powerful story in the world than your own personal testimony. The story of your salvation. For it involves God's supernatural resurrection power, His ability to raise the dead. Even with their millions of dollars and state-of-the-art CGI, Hollywood can't touch your supernatural testimony. Having been made alive in Christ, you are now an organic member of His bride, the Church. His body here on earth. Your significance finds its source and is derived from His. For apart from Him you can do nothing, but in Christ you can do all things.

As pastor and author Louie Giglio said about our Christian testimony:

"People say all the time 'I don't have a good testimony' because they think their story has to involve some dramatic story of change from 'bad' to 'good.' But Jesus didn't come to save people this way. Sin doesn't make us bad it makes us dead. Jesus came to save by bringing the dead to life. And that's an amazing testimony."

Your Story Matters: By Faith We Live

"Though the fig tree may not blossom, nor fruit be on the vines; though the labor of the olive may fail, and the fields yield no food; though the flock may be cut off from the fold, and there be no herd in the stalls – yet I will rejoice in the Lord, I will joy in the God of my salvation. The Lord God is my strength; He will make my feet like deer's feet, and He will make me walk on my high hills" (Habakkuk 3:17-19).

In the end, puzzled by God's apparent lack of answer to his prayers, and then when answered the answer itself, Habakkuk reaches a conclusion that is one of the most profound expressions of faith in the Bible. Even though we read about his fear in verse 16, that fear becomes surpassed by his faith in verses 17-19. *The just shall live* (thrive and flourish) *by his faith"* (Habakkuk 2:4). In the face of an invading army, Habakkuk declares the Lord is his invincible army. Brought to the end of his spiritual, mental, and emotional rope, our prophet found his courage and bravery not in himself or his resources, but in God alone.

It reminds us of Jehoshaphat in 2 Chronicles 20. Faced with similar prospects of an overwhelming enemy arriving soon, he too trembled *"And Jehoshaphat feared…"*. But he didn't stop there. *"And Jehoshaphat feared, and set himself to seek the Lord, and proclaimed a fast throughout all Judah"* (2 Chronicles 20:3). Before the deliverance, and stripped of all human solutions, the King in prayer cried out for help *"For we have no power against this great multitude that is coming against us; nor do we know what to do, but our eyes are upon You"* (2 Chronicles 20:12). Faith surpassed his fear.

And it reminds us of the children of Israel and their forty years of wandering in the desert. Although they too received the good news of the gospel, those desert nomads missed a critical ingredient: *"For indeed the gospel was preached to us as well as to them; but the word which they heard did not profit them, not being mixed with faith in those who heard it"* (Hebrews 4:2). They heard the gospel but did not believe it. They believed their circumstances. We, on the other hand, are *"… those who believe to the saving of the soul"* (Hebrews 10:39). Like Habakkuk, our faith won't make much human sense, and it will certainly not be our natural reaction, but that is just the point, *"For we walk by faith, not by sight"* (2 Corinthians 5:7).

Your Story Matters:
By Faith We Worship

"Yet I will rejoice in the Lord. I will joy in the God of my salvation"
(Habakkuk 3:18).

The Chaldeans are coming. There will be no fruit and no harvest. All the labor will come to naught. There will be no food, and all the flocks will be gone. Insert normal human reaction of fear here! That was the predicament facing Habakkuk. Having received an answer to his prayers, the prophet now accurately sees into the future. He knows what's about to occur, and it's not pretty. Unlike most of us who can only hypothesize about the future, Habakkuk knew beyond a shadow of a doubt. And what was his reaction? Or, more accurately, what was his intentional response?

Even though his situation and circumstances had not improved and, in fact, were about to become much worse, Habakkuk was gripped with unspeakable awe and a profound sense of security in His God. This decision of faith in Him produced action — it produced the deliberate choice to worship. *"I will rejoice... I will joy..."* He chose to trust in Him, to make the Lord God his anchor. Not in his investments, employment, retirement account, or any other earthly security. He knew God would meet him as he rejoices. He knew God lived in his praises – rejoicing in God would usher in His very comforting presence.

Like Paul and Silas praying and singing hymns while shackled in an inner prison (Acts 16:24-25). Or Paul, when once again he found himself imprisoned, could say, *"Rejoice in the Lord always. Again, I will say rejoice!"* (Philippians 4:4). Or the psalmist who spoke to his discouraged soul, *"Why are you cast down, O my soul? And why are you disquieted within me? Hope in God, for I shall yet praise Him"* (Psalm 42:5).

From the hymn *Though Troubles Assail Us*:

Though troubles assail us, and dangers affright,
Though friends should all fail us, and foes all unite,
Yet one thing secures us, whatever betide,
The promise assures us, "The Lord Will Provide."

When Satan assails us to stop up our path,
And courage all fails us, we triumph by faith.
He cannot take from us, though oft he has tried,
This heart-cheering promise, "The Lord Will Provide."

Your Story Matters: By Faith We Hope

"Though the fig tree may not blossom, nor fruit be on the vines; though the labor of the olive may fail, and the fields yield no food; though the flock may be cut off from the fold, and there be no herd in the stalls – yet I will rejoice in the Lord, I will joy in the God of my salvation. The Lord God is my strength; He will make my feet like deer's feet, and He will make me walk on my high hills" (Habakkuk 3:17-19).

From a human perspective, the couple had run out of hope. Having exhausted all the earthly hopes the medical community of their day could provide, infertility seemed to be their final destination. And yet, there was that promise the Lord made to the husband twenty-five years earlier, *"I will make you a great nation; and in you all the families of the earth shall be blessed"* (Genesis 12:2-3). Personalize that tension for your own life: A promise from God, disappointment every month for twenty-five long years, and still nothing. Would we still have hope based on a promise made so many years earlier?

Abraham did. But not the hope of this world. Another kind of hope. A resurrecting hope in a supernatural God who always keeps His promises. *"God, who gives life to the dead and calls those things which do not exist as though they did; who, contrary to hope, in hope believed, so that he became the father of many nations, according to what was spoken"* (Romans 4:17-18). Contrary to hope in hope, Abraham believed: This is what it means to trust God. To not just *know* His promises, but to *believe* His promises. Independent of circumstances. *"He did not waver at the promise of God through unbelief, but was strengthened in faith, giving glory to God, and being fully convinced that what He had promised He was also able to perform"* (Romans 4:20-21). What Jesus said to the desperate father He says to us today, *"If you can believe, all things are possible to him who believes"* (Mark 9:23). And like the father, if you are like me, we reply, *"Lord, I believe; help my unbelief!"* (Mark 9:24).

Jesus Christ, our living hope. All other earthly hopes have a finite lifespan and come to an ultimate end. Just as Habakkuk had come to realize. But a shift had occurred in him, and now contrary to hope in hope he believed. May that same shift occur in us today. *"Now may the God of hope fill you with all joy and peace in believing, that you may abound in hope by the power of the Holy Spirit"* (Romans 15:13).

Your Story Matters: By Faith We Are Victorious

"But the just shall live by his faith" (Habakkuk 2:4).

"The Lord God is my strength; He will make my feet like deer's feet, and He will make me walk on my high hills" (Habakkuk 3:19).

More than an attempt at an inspirational adage for this devotional, it's true: Faith is actually how we live and walk out the victorious Christian life. Here, Habakkuk chooses not to be under his mountains but is empowered to walk over them. *"He will make me walk on my high hills."* Habakkuk is going over and not under! The Amplified version of verse 19 says, *"The Lord God is my Strength, my personal bravery, and my invincible army; He makes my feet like hind's feet and will make me walk and make spiritual progress upon my high places."* Not only will Habakkuk be walking over his mountains, but he'll be making spiritual progress too! Do you know what the term spiritual progress means? "The state in which the born-again child of God enjoys and finds satisfaction in God's favor and salvation, regardless of his or her outward conditions." This is what it means to walk by faith!

1 John 5:4-5 explicitly declares our faith *is* the victory: *"For whatever is born of God overcomes the world.* **And this is the victory that has overcome the world – our faith.** *Who is he who overcomes the world, but he who believes that Jesus is the Son of God."*

Ephesians 6:10-18 tells us how to win, and what armor to wear on the spiritual battlefield of life. One necessary component is our shield of faith. In fact, we're told to bring it *above all*: *"Above all,* **taking up the shield of faith,** *with which you will be able to quench all the fiery darts of the wicked one."*

And Paul, at the end of his life here on earth, would victoriously declare, *"I have fought the good fight, I have finished the race,* **I have kept the faith**" (2 Timothy 4:7).

So this was how Habakkuk would walk in victory. *" But the just shall* **live by his faith.**" And this is why Peter would conclude, *"For a little while, if need be, you have been grieved by various trials, that the genuineness of* **your faith, being much more precious than gold** *that perishes, though it is tested by fire, may be found to praise, honor, and glory at the revelation of Jesus Christ, whom having not seen you love" (1 Peter 1:6-8).*

Soon and very soon, our faith will turn to sight, and we will forever see the One we love and adore, our Lord and Savior Jesus Christ.

Works Cited

Ortlund, Dane C. (2020) *Gentle and Lowly*, Wheaton, IL: Crossway. pp. 35-36.

Jennings, Marianne M. (2011) *Business Ethics: Case Studies and Readings,* Mason, OH: Cengage Learning. pp 133.

Lefcoe, George. (December 18, 1998) "Notable, Quotable" *Wall Street Journal.* Retrieved May 10, 2024 from https://www.wsj.com/articles/SB913938006533462000

Brooks, Arthur C. (2022) *From Strength to Strength*, New York, NY: Portfolio/Penguin. pp 207.

The Works of Ralph Waldo Emerson, in 12 vols. Fireside Edition *(Boston and New York, 1909).* Vol. 2 Essays. First Series. Retrieved April 12, 2024 from https://oll.libertyfund.org/titles/emerson-the-works-of-ralph-waldo-emerson-vol-2-essays-first-series

Tirabassi, Becky. (2010) *Change Your Life Daily Bible,* Carol Stream, IL Tyndale House Publishers. pp 245 and 302.

Balk, Gene. (October 12, 2023) "People without college degrees increasingly rare in Seattle" *The Seattle Times.* Retrieved March 28, 2024 from https://www.seattletimes.com/seattle-news/data/people-without-college-degrees-increasingly-rare-in-seattle/

Rigney, Joe. (April 16, 2014) "When Envy Turns Deadly" *desiringGod.* Retrieved April 10, 2024 from https://www.desiringgod.org/articles/when-envy-turns-deadly

Weaver, Joanna. (2022) *Embracing Trust* Grand Rapids, MI: Revell/Baker Publishing Group. pp. 127-141.

Rameer, Vanessa Mae. (January 16, 2024) "US Loneliness Statistics 2024: Are Americans Lonely?" *Science of People.* Retrieved May 3, 2024 from https://www.scienceofpeople.com/loneliness-statistics/

McGinty, Mike. (August 17, 2021) "Japan Appoints Minister of Loneliness, Can He Solve The Loneliness Problem?" *OMF United States.* Retrieved March 11, 2024 from https://omf.org/us/japan-appoints-minister-of-loneliness-can-he-solve-the-loneliness-problem/Comer, John Mark. (2024) *Practicing the Way.* Colorado Springs, CO: Waterbrook. p 59

Peterson, Skye. Getty, Keith. Getty, Krysten. (2022) "Take Shelter" *Christ Our Hope In Life And Death.* Getty Music.

Raglin, Tim. (2021) "Cost of Not Changing: The Tyranny of the Urgent" *Skillwork.* Retrieved February 26, 2024 from https://resources.skillwork.com/cost-of-not-changing-the-tyranny-of-the-urgent

Brooks, David. (2016) *The Road to Character* New Your, NY: Random House. p 11.

"Gold Rush at Costco" Uploaded April 3, 2024 https://www.today.com/video/costco-is-selling-up-to-200-million-worth-of-gold-bars-every-month-208771141620

Gingerich, Barton. (November 20, 2018) "Shenandoah and 'every good gift' for which we give thanks" *Religion and Liberty Online.* Retrieved April 29, 2024 from https://rlo.acton.org/archives/104781-shenandoah-and-every-good-gift-for-which-we-give-thanks.html

"An Introduction to the Book of Habakkuk", *Bible.org.* Retrieved February 8, 2024 from https://bible.org/article/introduction-book-habakkuk

Lloyd-Jones, D. Martyn. (1982) *From Fear to Faith: Studies in the Book of Habakkuk.* Ada, MI: Baker Publishing Group.

Nouwen, Henri (August 12, 2023) "We are Seen by God's Loving Eyes" *Henri Nouwen Society.* Retrieved April 10, 2024 from https://henrinouwen.org/meditations/we-are-seen-by-gods-loving-eyes/

"When and how was Israel conquered by the Assyrians?" *Got Questions.* Retrieved January 30, 2024 from https://www.gotquestions.org/Israel-conquered-by-Assyria.html

Yancy, Phillip. (1988) *Disappointment with God.* Grand Rapids MI: Zondervan.

Voskamp, Anne. (2011) *One Thousand Gifts.* Nashville, TN: HarperCollins Christian Publishing.

Brandeis, Louis. (May 26, 2009) "Brandeis and the History of Transparency" *Sunlight Foundation.* Retrieved May 3, 2024 from https://sunlightfoundation.com/2009/05/26/brandeis-and-the-history-of-transparency/

Grierson, Tim. (2020) "How 'Na Na Hey Hey Kiss Him Goodbye' Became The Song We Use To Taunt Our Opponents At Sporting Events". *MEL.* Retrieved June 10, 2024 from https://melmagazine.com/en-us/story/how-na-na-hey-hey-kiss-him-goodbye-became-the-song-we-use-to-taunt-our-opponents-at-sporting-events

"The Power of Story" *National Geographic.* Retrieved April 17, 2024 from https://www.nationalgeographic.org/society/storytellers-collective/the-power-of-story/#:~:text=People%20remember%20how%20stories%20make,and%20share%20them%20with%20others.

Giglio, Louie. (June 3, 2024) "The Power of Your Personal Story" *The 260 Journey.* Retrieved on June 18, 2024 from https://260journey.com/the-power-of-your-personal-story/

Ware, Bronnie. (2012) The Top Five Regrets of the Dying. Carlsbad, CA: Hay House Inc.

Lacriox, Eva. (April 7, 2021) "Marketers Beware, using envy in advertising may push consumers to a competitor brand" Bayes Business School. Retrieved April 28, 2024 https://www.bayes.city.ac.uk/news-and-events/news/2021/april/envy-in-marketing

Hewitt, Felix. (March 20, 2024) "The Fastest Human: How Fast Can Usain Bolt Run? Marathon Handbook. Retrieved May 10, 2024 https://marathonhandbook.com/how-fast-can-usain-bolt-run

"Martin Luther Quotable Quotes" goodreads Retrieved March 3, 2024 https://www.goodreads.com/quotes/878756

Lee, Eunia. "You Complete Me": An Examination of Marital Expectations" Stenzel Clinical Services. Retrieved January 27, 2024 https://stenzelclinical.com/complete/

"Mehrabian's 7-38-55 Communication Model" World of Work Project. Retrieved April 1, 2024 https://worldofwork.io/2019/07/mehrabians-7-38-55-communication-model

"Elisabeth Elliot Quotes" goodreads Retrieved June 5, 2024 https://www.goodreads.com/author/quotes/6264.

"C. S. Lewis Quotable Quotes" goodreads Retrieved June 5, 2024 https://www.goodreads.com/quotes/6439

"Mariana Trench" Britannica Retrieved January 16, 2024 https://www.britannica.com/place/Mariana-Trench

Bible Study Resources for Women

Flourish Through the Word is a unique community created for women to study the Bible together, further cultivating their friendship with Jesus and with one another.

We come together in community as a large group for Bible teaching and worship, and then meet as small groups in homes on alternating weeks. As women come together to share their Bible study findings in this setting, friendships are a natural result. Women pray for each other, share their hearts through the Word of God, and spur one another on in their daily walks with Jesus.

Each study is designed to be an equipping tool for women of all ages to dive deeper into the Word as they complete it on a short-term basis (10-12 weeks).

As women find deeper friendship centered on the Word of God, they can't help but flourish! Visit us at *www.flourishthroughtheword.com*.

A five-week journey on grace, truth, the Holy Spirit, and our identity, starting with the Gospel of John.

Spend four weeks on biblical principles of friendship, exploring commitment, communication, and community through Scripture.

Explore 1 Peter, focusing on faith, hope, love, and practical Christian living through a five-week personal study.

The letter of 2 Peter focuses on spiritual disciplines and intentional growth through Jesus' provision for living in truth.

A six-week study on how God's Word transforms us, guiding us to flourish spiritually and joyfully.

Learn how investing in others and recognizing their worth through biblical disciple-making principles is a life-giving key.

A seven-week study inviting deeper relationship with God through biblical stories, declarations, and gratitude journaling.

This five-week study in James focuses on practical wisdom and spiritual growth through daily biblical reflection.

Explore how personal stories fit into God's Kingdom by studying the book of Habakkuk and the life of David.

This five-week study examines biblical stories of faith and courage, offering encouragement and guidance for facing fear.

This six-week study highlights the bravery of Abraham, Mary, the mother of Jesus, Peter and John, Paul and Silas, King David, and the woman at the well.

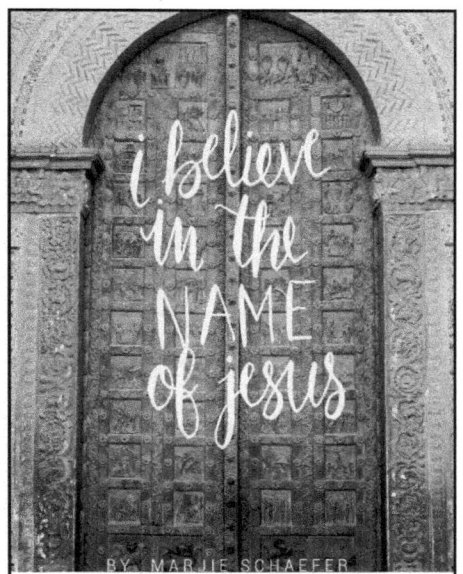

A study of the seven "I Am" statements of Jesus, exploring their significance and impact.

Walk through the book of Ephesians, focusing on Christ's majesty and practical daily living through Paul's biblical prayers and teachings.

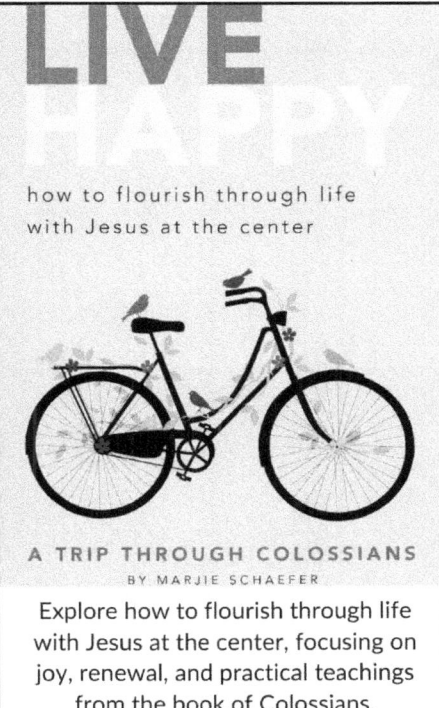

Explore how to flourish through life with Jesus at the center, focusing on joy, renewal, and practical teachings from the book of Colossians.

A four-week study of Philippians, teaching how to find true joy through gratitude and knowing Jesus as we rise above our circumstances by grace.

Other Devotional Readings from Steve & Marjie Schaefer

www.ingramcontent.com/pod-product-compliance
Lightning Source LLC
Chambersburg PA
CBHW061738070526
44585CB00024B/2718